interviewing
skills
for
managers

D0609960

interviewing

skills

for

managers

A step-by-step guide to conducting successful workplace interviews

Tony and Gillian Pont

PIATKUS

Copyright © 1998 by Tony Pont and Gillian Pont

All rights reserved

First published in Great Britain in 1998 by
Judy Piatkus (Publishers) Ltd
5 Windmill Street
London W1P 1HF

This paperback edition published in 1998

The moral rights of the authors have been asserted

*A catalogue record for this book is available
from the British Library*

ISBN 0 7499 1780 6 hbk
ISBN 0 7499 1882 9 pbk

Typeset by Action Typesetting Ltd, Gloucester
Printed and bound in Great Britain by
The Bath Press, Bath

To Simon and Nicholas

EVESHAM COLLEGE
LIBRARY

| CLASS NUMBER | 658,31124 |
| ACCESSION NUMBER | 017485 |

Contents

Introduction

Virtually everybody, on every day of their lives, conducts an interview of sorts. At the simplest level it will just be asking a question to elicit information in a very informal setting. The ability to ask questions, clarify understanding and engage in a positive interaction with someone else are vital skills in the communication process.

In the workplace, changing trends in responsibilities and roles, coupled with changes in attitudes and behaviours, have combined to ensure that most managers will become increasingly involved in more formal interviewing. The days of the remote boss, locked behind closed doors, rarely seen and frequently inaccessible, have been replaced by a more open-door, participative, team-oriented style of managing, requiring a much higher degree of interpersonal skill. Furthermore, with many organisations engaged in a process of 'downsizing' or 'delayering', more and more line managers are taking on greater responsibility for 'people issues'. What was once seen as the responsibility of Personnel or Human Resources is now seen as the responsibility of the line manager. In addition to the usual responsibility or involvement in the selection process, many managers are expected to conduct appraisals, career counselling or other counselling duties, and may also be the contact point with their work area's customers, handling customer complaints from time to time. All of this, therefore, has demanded a different set of management skills from those of yesteryear.

This book is aimed at the manager who is largely

untrained and inexperienced in interview techniques. However, interviewing is a multi-faceted set of skills, with different emphases according to situation. As there is now such a wide range of workplace interviews, no manager will be skilled and competent in all. This book will therefore be invaluable to all managers, regardless of your skills and experience.

For the inexperienced manager, there are many things that can go wrong in an interview. When they do, not only is the result a bad interview, but often the manager creates a bad image of him or herself, and of the organisation, in the eyes of the interviewee. The true cost of a poorly conducted interview has never been, and can never be, computed, which is why some managers tend to be dismissive of such procedures, either ignoring their own performance and the damage done, or just putting it down to experience. If poorly conducted interviews and interactions had a direct and measurable impact on a manager's budget and bottom line, then managers would be less dismissive of their own shortcomings.

Our research among numerous managers has indicated that the following reasons are why managers fail to carry out an effective interview:

- they don't plan and prepare
- they haven't clarified in their own mind exactly what their objectives are
- they don't ask the right questions
- they don't listen
- they don't seek and clarify the relevant information
- they possess poor interpersonal skills
- they haven't dealt with their own emotions and agendas
- they find decision-making difficult.

Whilst there is no magic formula to becoming a

skilful and effective interviewer, most, if not all, of us can become competent, largely by addressing the reasons for ineffectiveness outlined above. To help you, wherever appropriate the chapters are structured into a Before, During and After format and the introductory chapter 1 takes you through the processes step by step. Chapter 1 looks in general terms at the range of communication skills used in interviewing and these are then given the appropriate slant in succeeding chapters when different communication skills need emphasis according to the type of interview conducted.

We cannot conclude the introduction without a brief word of thanks to those people who have contributed in no small way to this book. Firstly, our thanks go to Edna Pollard for typing the manuscript in her usual efficient manner. Secondly, our thanks to the numerous individuals who, over the years, in a variety of interview situations, have provided shining examples of how to, and how not to, conduct an interview. They have made the theory come alive and provided a wonderful vehicle for learning; we hope that others will learn from our experiences and become more confident and competent interviewers.

interviewing
skills
for
managers

1

General Skills of Interviewing

'Would you please tell me please, which way
I ought to go from here?'
'That depends a good deal on where you want
to get to.'
Alice's Adventures in Wonderland

There are numerous definitions of interviews, but most, if not all of them, have a number of common characteristics. These characteristics are:

- a face-to-face meeting (with the exception of telephone interviews)
- a meeting with a specific purpose or objective
- a two-way exchange of information.

As this book will show, there are several different types of interview, which can be conducted with varying degress of formality or informality in a variety of settings. These include:

Type of interview	Aim
Selection	To choose the most suitable person for the job, from a range of applicants.
Appraisal	To review the interviewee's performance and to agree ways to enhance this in the future.

Disciplinary	To explore a possible performance problem or breach of regulations and to take the appropriate action.
Counselling	To help the interviewee identify and solve their own problems, which could be either work-related or personal.

Certain fundamental skills and techniques are common to all types of interview, or can be modified accordingly, and it is these general skills which will be the focus of this chapter.

Interviews – the benefits and problems

Interviews are just one way of giving and gathering information, along with questionnaires, tests, written exercises and reports and references. However, interviews offer a number of significant advantages over the other methods and it is these that account for their popularity and importance. The benefits for the interviewer are as follows:

Because interviews are:	**The interviewer is able to:**
Face-to-face	establish/maintain rapport and develop/maintain interest
	gauge various subjective things such as personality, relationships, etc.
	'read between the lines' and understand the message rather than just hear/read the words.

Interactive   check the understanding of
                               all parties concerned
                               verify information by asking
                               questions in different ways
                               probe for supplementary
                               information where necessary.

However, the same features that offer these benefits
can also create numerous problems, so that, if poorly
conducted, the benefits of the interview can be nulli-
fied. For an interview to be conducted effectively, the
interviewer needs to be aware of the potential pitfalls in
order to avoid or overcome them.

Because interviews are: **These problems can occur:**
Interactive and   Interviews can be costly as
face-to-face   they take up a significant slot
                               of time on both sides.
                               The success of the interview
                               relies heavily on the skill of the
                               interviewer. If the interviewer
                               makes assumptions, doesn't
                               check and probe for
                               information by skilful
                               questioning, is moody or
                               doesn't listen well, the outcome
                               can be less than reliable.
                               The interviewer's prejudice
                               or hidden agenda can affect
                               their judgment (the bias may
                               be positive or negative).
                               The interviewer may influ-
                               ence the interviewee through
                               their attitudes, expectations,
                               tone of voice, expressions,
                               leading questions, etc.

All these problems impact upon the success of the interview in varying degrees of importance according to the type of interview being conducted. As a result, the benefits of flexibility and spontaneity can be lost and the effectiveness of the interview reduced by the intruding bias or poor technique.

How can interviews be made more effective?

The answer to this question is to plan and prepare, and conduct the interview by using the appropriate communication skills. To improve our chances of success we need to follow a systematic approach which is outlined as follows, by considering the following:

(a) Defining the aims of the interview.
(b) Defining the objectives of the interview.
(c) What do I need to plan for in terms of questions, resources and design?
(d) What is the content of the interview to be?
(e) What do I need to do while actually conducting the interview?
(f) How can the interview be evaluated and followed up?
(g) How can I get better in the future?

The sequence is shown diagramatically in Figure 1.1.

(a) Defining the aims

One is often asked, 'What is the difference between an aim and an objective?' In general, the aim represents the overall goal of the interview. As with most things, the interviewer needs to know what he/she is trying to achieve in order to have a reasonable chance of being successful. With this in mind, the very first questions the interviewer should ask before conducting the interview are:

Fig. 1.1 The systematic approach to interviewing

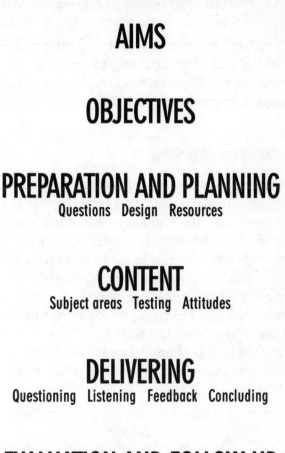

AIMS

OBJECTIVES

PREPARATION AND PLANNING
Questions   Design   Resources

CONTENT
Subject areas   Testing   Attitudes

DELIVERING
Questioning   Listening   Feedback   Concluding

EVALUATION AND FOLLOW-UP
Self Interview   Contract with interviewee

END GOALS

'Why am I going to conduct this interview?'
and
'What do I want to achieve?'

These two questions will help to decide on the overall aim, which will vary according to circumstances, type of interview, etc. Some more examples of the aims of an interview were mentioned on pages 1–2.

(b) Defining the objectives

An objective is a precise goal stated in clear, measurable, quantitative or qualitative terms so that at the end of the interview the interviewer can quickly and easily assess whether the objectives were achieved. They will also provide *one* reference point in evaluating the effectiveness of the interview. In formulating objectives, the interviewer must first clearly identify the overall aim of the interview and then ask, 'What things do I need to do in order to achieve my aim?'

Using the appraisal interview as an example, the relationship between aims and objectives would be as follows:

Aim	Objectives
To review the interviewee's performance and to agree how this can be enhanced.	To discuss the interviewee's performance (good and poor aspects) over the last twelve months. To identify the individual's strengths and how he/she can capitalise on these. To identify the individual's weaknesses and to develop a plan to address them.

To discuss how our working relationship can be further developed.

(c) Preparing for the interview

As with all interactive situations, the cliché 'failing to plan is planning to fail' is applicable to interviews. Expecting just to turn up and conduct the interview can, at worst, result in an unmitigated disaster. The interviewer must prepare and plan and this requires a similar investment of time to that spent in the interview room. The amount of time spent preparing and planing will vary according to circumstance. Important variables are experience and expertise. Generally the lower these two are, the more time needs to be spent preparing. As a rule of thumb, the inexperienced interviewer should operate on the basis of preparation time to interview time being at a 3:1 ratio. Experienced and competent interviewers must guard against complacency and the ratio of preparation time to interview time should, at worst, be 1:1; a better ratio would be nearer 2:1.

What, then, are some of the tasks that the interviewer can do beforehand in order to minimise the chances of failure and to maximise the chances of conducting an effective interview? The tasks that should be carried out are as follows:

Read through all appropriate and important documentation
These are some examples of the kind of documentation you might consult:

Type of interview	Documentation
Selection	Application form, CV, references, letter of application, job specification, test results.

Appraisal	Previous appraisal documentation.
Disciplinary	The organisation's disciplinary procedure. Written evidence of performance problems.
Counselling	Case notes.

Decide what information the interview is to provide

For an interview to be effective you need to collect, and give, the necessary information in the time allowed. To do this, you need to *know* what information you are trying to collect. Information for information's sake has little value. Therefore, during your preparation, focus your thoughts on what you really *need* to know. Once you have identified this relevant information, you will be able to review progress during the interview and recognise when you have achieved your objectives. To help do this it is useful to record, in one form or another, some of the major headings and individual points that can be ticked off as the interview proceeds. This ensures that at the end of the interview you have covered everything you wanted to cover and avoids self-recriminations: 'I wish I had asked that.' It is important to get it right first time.

Once you have decided what information you will be covering, you can think about how the topics link together. This will help you create a logical sequence to the interview, although the flow should be flexible in response to the interviewee's information, rather than rigid.

Create an appropriate environment

The setting in which interviews are conducted can have a dramatic effect upon the outcome. With careful thought and preparation of the room and the conditions, you can create a more relaxed atmosphere for interviewing which, for the *majority* of interviews, should be your intention.

Layout

Ask yourself these main questions about the layout of the room:

- Is there adequate room available? (The room should be neither too large nor too small.)
- Is a table necessary? (Be aware of the barrier this can create.)
- Where should the table be in relation to the chairs? (Consider distance, position and elevation.)
- Are the chairs of similar height, comfort, etc.? (Differential seating can create feelings of superiority and inadequacy.)
- How close/far away should you be seated?
- What relative positions should the chairs be in? (Side by side, face to face, or somewhere in between?)

Below are a number of seating arrangements used in interview situations. Listed alongside are some of the effects (advantages and disadvantages) of each arrangement, and the types of interview in which they are used.

X X X X

- Often used in promotion boards, panel selection interviews and disciplinary hearings.
- Very formal and can be intimidating for the interviewee, so much so that they can give wrong impressions, can cause interviewee to 'freeze'.

X

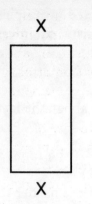

- Used in some Selection Interviews.
- Distance creates formality and sometimes poor interaction. Is often used by interviewers who feel threatened or are insecure and need the space and table to create a barrier behind which they can hide.

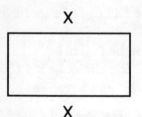

- Used in some Selection, Disciplinary and Appraisal Interviews.
- The desk creates a barrier between the two parties – a 'them' and 'me' mentality.
- Often used by interviewers who feel insecure and wish to hide behind rank. This can be exacerbated if the interviewee's chair is smaller and at a lower level.

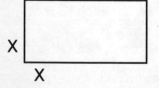

- Much less formal and confrontational than the previous seating arrangements.
- Usually creates easier interactions.
- Can be a good arrangement for Appraisal, Feedback and Selection Interviews when a horizontal surface is required for paperwork.

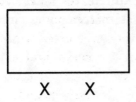

- Encourages greater informality and moves away from some of the more confrontational seating arrangements.
- The two parties can either be face to face or, if referring to paperwork, shoulder to shoulder.
- Very useful arrangement for feedback of test and exam results.

- Seating arrangement informal and non-confrontational.
- Interactions likely to be informal and friendly; encourages openness.
- A low coffee table between the two parties, especially if used for refreshments, can increase informality.
- Such arrangement in a very large room can reduce informality.
- Suitable for Selection, Appraisal and Counselling Interviews.

In the above six seating arrangements, you will have realised that the degree of formality decreases from extreme formality in the first arrangement to informality in the last three arrangements. Consequently, the early seating arrangements are more suited to Disciplinary and some Selection Interviews (especially panel interviews) and the later ones for Feedback, Counselling and Appraisal Interviews. We advise you to select the arrangement best suited to meet your comfort needs, while ensuring it matches your interview objectives.

Conditions
Consider the following:

- Is the room temperature comfortable?
- Is the room light enough? Certainly try to avoid a dingy room. Try to aim for a well-lit room, lit by natural light.
- Will the sunshine trouble either of you? Neither party should be squinting in the bright glare of the sun. It is not an interrogation!
- Is there adequate ventilation? A room that is too stuffy can reduce energy and induce drowsiness.

Interruptions and distractions
- Is the room private and free from interruptions by other people or by phone? Have arrangements been made for the interception of incoming calls?
- Is the surface of the desk/table tidy?
- Is the decor of the room pleasant but conservative?

All these three factors can either focus the mind or cause it to wander.

Time
- Has sufficient time been allowed? Always err on the side of being generous with the time allocation. You can't be certain of how the interview will develop and anxiety over time is usually communicated to the interviewee.
- Is the appointed time convenient for all parties?
- Is a clock clearly visible? This may be necessary if you are running to a tight schedule. Interviewers should

try to avoid looking obviously at their wrist watch –
it often gives the wrong message.

• As a general rule, 20–50 minutes is usually adequate
and we advise you not to exceed one hour.

All the above environmental factors can be easily
controlled and make an enormous contribution to a
successful and effective interview. Moreover, once the
right environment has been prepared, the interviewer
can give the interviewee their full attention.

(d) Content

Remember the main principles and structure of an interview.

Interviews can be broken down into three main stages
– a beginning, a middle and an end – each of which has
its own underlying theme and major activities. This is
outlined below.

Stage and theme	Activities
Beginning: Introduction	Introductions. Create rapport. Put interviewee at ease. Explain purpose of interview (and sequence).
Middle: Gathering and giving information through questioning and discussion	Cover 'safe' subjects first. Give interviewee encouragement. Probe for information and listen carefully to the answers and investigate where required. Check for understanding (both ways). Take notes if helpful.

Confront problems that are raised – don't avoid them.
Judge impartially – avoid bias.
Give information clearly and succinctly.
Summarise and reflect at regular intervals.
Invite questions.

End: Summary and conclusion   Recap on what has been agreed.

Although the emphasis given to each stage may vary according to the circumstances, the underlying principles remain the same.

Whilst there are distinct stages to an interview, it is important to make the interview flow smoothly, both within a topic area and from topic to topic. If a logical sequence can be developed through the interview, the interviewee will be more relaxed and therefore more willing and able to answer the questions. However, if the interviewer jumps from topic to topic and back again, it is very likely that the interviewee will find this confusing, irritating and/or unsettling and this can impair the outcome of the interview.

Having identified the information that needs to be collected (section (c) above), thought should be given to how it all links together – is there a natural sequence, e.g. a chronological order or a series of similar events to explore? Look for connections and links to form a bridge from one topic to another. For example, in a Selection Interview, if the subject under discussion is the candidate's hectic job, the interviewer can guide the conversation towards hobbies by saying, 'You seem to have an extremely busy job. What opportunity do you get for leisure activities?' Or, 'Having said you find your job very demanding, what do you do for relaxation?'

Another example of linking topics would be from talking about the terms and conditions the applicant's current company offers (e.g. sick pay, annual holiday entitlement, free private medical insurance, etc.) to talking about whether they have had much sickness absence recently, or how they have spent their annual leave. Or, in an Appraisal Interview, the interviewer can lead the conversation from giving recognition to the subordinate's strengths to identifying weaknesses by saying, 'You certainly directed the XYZ project very capably, but do you think there are any parts you could have done better?'

By identifying possible links before the interview, it is easier to recognise and respond to them if and when the interviewee mentions them. It is important to remember that the link doesn't have to be picked upon as soon as it is raised, but, just by recognising it, the interviewer can refer back to it when ready. For example, 'Perhaps I could pick up a point you mentioned earlier. You said ... What did you learn from that experience?' In this way, even though there has been a change of subject, the interviewee has been given the opportunity to 'tune-in' in to the new topic in readiness for subsequent questions.

Allow some flexibility in the interview and don't be a slave to a planned sequence – even though your sequence may seem logical, this view may not be shared by the interviewee.

(e) Delivering the interview

Several skills are called upon in conducting an interview, all of which can be grouped under the heading

Communication Skills. In the interview situation these are mainly:

- questioning skills
- skills of active listening
- skills of appropriate body language or non-verbal communication (NVC).

All these skills need to be displayed by both the interviewer and the interviewee, the emphasis varying according to role; but the focus here will be on the interviewer. Remember also that it is the interviewer who sets the tone of the interview, so it is important that the appropriate behaviour and skills are displayed. Remember the old cliché 'behaviour breeds behaviour': the interviewee will, consciously or subconsciously, tend to behave in the same way as you, whether you are behaving appropriately or inappropriately.

In this section we will look at the communication process before discussing further the main communication skills required by the interviewer.

Communication skills

Communication can be defined as 'the process of transferring ideas or thoughts from one person to another, for the purpose of creating understanding in the person receiving the communication'. Although every day we communicate hundreds of times, misunderstandings frequently occur. It is important to recognise just how many problems can occur with communication and that some of these will take place in the mind, even before a word has been spoken. In fact, when one considers the number of factors that can, and do, interfere with the communication process, it is amazing that any effective communication takes place!

Any communication must involve a minimum of two people – the sender and the receiver. In the role of interviewer, remember that while you should aim to be talking for only about 20% of the time, you are communicating as both the sender *and* the receiver, so let's view the communication process from both perspectives.

Firstly, as the sender, try to avoid confusion or misunderstandings by:

i) Working at sending clear, unambiguous messages.
    Think about your use of words, the logic of the message, whether it has been pitched at an appropriate level, and your body language (does it support the message or are conflicting messages being sent)? And:

ii) Checking that the message has been understood as it was intended to be.
    Ask the interviewee to summarise, listen to what they are saying, and watch how they respond.

Secondly, as the receiver, try to avoid misunderstandings by:

i) Actively listening to what is being said.
    Concentrate and work at listening, not just at interview but in everyday life. Listening techniques are discussed later in this chapter, and again in chapter 4. Like all communication skills, practice makes perfect, or at the very least brings about improvement. Also:

ii) Observing any non-verbal behaviour.
    Consider the implications.

iii) Asking for clarification of any unclear verbal and non-verbal messages.

iv) Summarising your understanding at regular intervals.

As interviewer, you have the responsibility both as speaker *and* as listener to ensure that your communication with the other person is effective. Fulfilling this responsibility is essential for an interview to be effective and it is a responsibility that *cannot* be shirked.

Questioning techniques

Clearly, good questioning techniques are extremely important in interviews. Skilful questioning can significantly enhance both the quantity and quality of information gathered. The questions should guide the conversation in the intended direction, for example to collect general information, to gather specific details or to probe for underlying reasons or feelings. By choosing the right questions to ask, the interviewer will be able to guide and control the interview unobtrusively, i.e. without talking too much. *The more time spent talking, the less opportunities there are to learn about the interviewee and gauge their reactions.*

There are four main types of question:

- Closed questions
- Leading questions
- Multiple questions
- Open questions:
  - Probes
  - Links

Closed questions

Closed questions are questions that will prompt a 'yes' or 'no' answer (they are sometimes called 'binary questions').

Closed questions are of limited value in all interviews for three reasons:

- The interviewer will do more of the talking than the interviewee: 'Did you take any examinations at school?' 'No.' As a result, the amount of information you are able to collect about the interviewee, in the time available, will be severely restricted.
- The interviewer will have little or no time to think of

the next question to ask. Very quickly the problem becomes compounded, as a vicious circle is established.
• The third problem with closed questions is that they are often based on assumptions. If your assumptions are wrong, the reply you receive can set both parties back: 'I take it that you enjoy your work?' 'No!'

So limit your use of closed questions. It may not be possible to avoid using them altogether as there will be certain facts that you will need to check.

e.g.   'When you left the company you were twenty-eight?'
       'Yes.'
       'And you didn't take up your new position until July 1997?'
       'Yes.'

If you unintentionally ask a closed question, follow it with an open question or probe:

e.g.   'Do you have any hobbies?'
       'Yes.'
       'What are they?'/'Why do you like orienteering?'/
       'What is the appeal of orienteering?'

Leading questions

Leading questions are questions that indicate the desired answer – hence their other name, 'loaded questions'. People have to be strong, or (if they want to 'pass' the interview) stupid, to give a different answer from the one that is being drawn from them. Some examples are:

    'Presumably you are ambitious?'
    'Punctuality is essential in this job – what is your time-keeping like?'
    'I assume you can use the word processors?'

Leading questions have *no* value at all and they should be avoided at all times.

Multiple questions

As the name implies, a multiple question is in fact a number of questions which have been strung together. For example, 'What is worrying you? Is it that your job will be jeopardised? Or is it the principle of the matter?'

It is often the case with multiple questions that the first question is the best question, i.e. an open question. However, the interviewee usually answers the *last* question, which is often a closed question, as in the example above. Or, the clever interviewee will choose the one they want to answer. Politicians, if fed multiple questions, often do this, thereby avoiding the issue they wish to avoid.

Multiple questions should be avoided – they only confuse the interviewee. If a multiple question slips out, then it is best to stop and ask *one* question that needs answering. For instance, in the above example you could follow on by saying, 'Perhaps I can rephrase that. What is it that is worrying you?' By doing this you are not taking pot-luck on which of your three questions the interviewee will answer.

Don't use multiple questions as a trick way of checking whether the interviewee can return to each of the questions in turn. Any type of trick questions will be counter-productive in that they will build an atmosphere of suspicion and possibly resentment. This is not conducive to an open or honest exchange of information.

Open questions

Open questions are the key to successful questioning technique. An open question is one that encourages the interviewee to talk; it's a question that *can't* be answered by 'yes' or 'no'! Open questions require the interviewee to give you information, opinions, feelings, and so on.

How, readers may enquire, do you ask an open question¿ To answer this open question, here's what Rudyard Kipling had to say:

Six Faithful Serving Men
I have six faithful serving men
They taught me all I know
Their names are What and Why and When
and How and Where and Who.

Other examples of open questions include:

'Tell me about ...'
'Please describe ...'
'Which way would you ...¿'
'Please would you illustrate that point ...'
'... and ... ¿'

Each of these questions calls for a descriptive answer and therefore offers the questioner the opportunity to listen and learn about the interviewee.

(i) Using open questions to probe for information
Probing for underlying feelings and opinions is essential in order to get a reasonable understanding of the interviewee. Open questions are ideal for probing – when you are given a short and/or superficial answer you can follow this up with: 'That's interesting. Why ...¿' or, 'What caused that ...¿' or, 'How did that affect you ...¿'

An interview should not appear to be an interrogation, so it is important for interviewers to give consideration to their non-verbal behaviour when asking open questions.

- Don't talk very fast.
- Don't stare.
- Do smile.
- Do show interest – be alert but not tense.
- Do acknowledge that you are listening to the interviewee, e.g. by nodding and making *quiet* noises such as 'uh huh ...', 'mmm ...', etc. This often encourages the interviewee to continue talking.

(ii) Using open questions to link topics

We have already discussed the importance of linking one subject to another and referring back to points that need to be probed further. Open questions are useful for this too. For example: 'You mentioned earlier that you want to work for an American company. Why is this?' Or, 'Having explained *why* you must work to these standards, what do you think you could do to improve your performance?'

By the careful use of questions, the interviewer can control the conversation and guide it in the direction they want.

(iii) Using pauses

> 'The right word may be effective, but no word was as effective as a rightly timed pause.'
> Mark Twain

The experienced interviewer can use the power of silence to encourage a further contribution from the interviewee. They can use it to indicate that more is expected. However, the danger with all powerful tools is that, inappropriately used, difficulties or damage can ensue. 'Awkward' silences or 'pregnant' pauses can cause embarrassment and therefore the interviewer needs acute sensitivity to the atmosphere and to the interviewee so that they can time their moment to resume control of the interview and avoid adverse reactions. The pause is probably more relevant to the Counselling Interview than to the other types of interview outlined in this book, although it does have applications in all types of interviews.

(iv) Guidelines for questioning
Good interviewers:

• Ask one question at a time.
• Ask open questions aimed at getting a particular piece of information.
• Use brief, simply worded and easily understandable questions.
• Don't make assumptions or prejudge the issue – they ask!
• Pitch questions at an appropriate level.
• Don't ask leading questions or try to catch someone out.
• Keep away from personal questions, except when necessary, and in that case explain why, and ask them in a detached way.
• Are patient and keep an open mind.
• Use self-control – keep off their hobby horses.
• Unobtrusively keep control and don't let the interviewee interview them.

Listening techniques
Having asked the right questions, the only way to do justice to the interviewee is to listen carefully to their answers. Studies have shown that we spend about 80% of our working hours communicating, 45% of which we spend listening. Inevitably these percentages will vary according to the situation – for example, while conducting an interview the percentage of time spent listening

would be far higher. Despite the fact that listening is a vitally important managerial skill, few of us have ever been taught *how* to listen more effectively. A major problem for most of us is that our minds are so full of our own thoughts and feelings that we pay little attention to what the other person really means, feels, needs and wants. We are all capable at one time or another of 'going on mental walkabout', preoccupied with our own agendas. The result is that often a very large percentage of what one person conveys to another is ignored, overlooked and wasted. Consequently people feel misunderstood and it is often not because they failed to express themselves clearly but because they were not listened to effectively. The skill which reduces the amount of misunderstanding is called *active listening* and, like all other communication skills, it can be improved with practice.

Active listening
Active listening involves concentrating on what the other person is saying in order to work out what it reveals about them and about what they really mean, feel, want and need; and then stating this back to them so they can check and confirm the accuracy of your understanding or correct any misunderstandings. In short, the message sent is the one received and understood.

This skill makes listening an *active* and not a *passive* activity because it requires the following:

- total *concentration*
- the mental effort of *interpreting* what the other person is saying
- *stating back* to the other person your interpretation of the message.

In interviews, a helpful technique is to *summarise*

what has been said from time to time – this helps the interviewer to recall the conversation and it helps both parties to check if they have understood and offers the opportunity for clarification if necessary. In addition, by summarising, you let the interviewee know that you have been listening to what has been said.

Another important technique is *reflecting*. Reflecting deals with the interviewee's feelings – which may or may not have been mentioned overtly. Recognising the interviewee's feelings builds empathy between the two parties. It will enhance your understanding of the person and what they are saying, and it also improves the chances of communicating effectively. If you find that the interviewee is experiencing strong feelings about certain issues, you can focus on the parts of the message which are important to *you*, the interviewer, which might otherwise get ignored or distorted.

An example of reflecting would be:

'I seem to be running around all the time trying to fulfil the needs of my staff rather than focusing on the work of the department.'
'Are you saying that you feel that you are under more than the usual amount of pressure at the moment?'
'Yes. I suppose I do.'

Reflecting, as you can see, means giving back a reflection of the feelings behind what the speaker has said. It is like a summary of feelings which have not been explicitly stated and is therefore different from 'summarising' which is a summary of the factual content. When reflecting, the listener acts as a mirror of the speaker's feelings, but doesn't pass comment or 'judge' those feelings.

Diagrammatically, the difference between Active and Passive listening is shown in Figure 1.2. To become a competent interviewer the skill of active listening has to be practised and developed. Look for every opportunity to do so. Like all communication skills, once is has been learned, you can apply it unconsciously to all interactive situations, not just interviewing.

Non-verbal communication (NVC)

The study of non-verbal communication (or body language) is a relatively recent phenomenon and researchers have noted and recorded about one million non-verbal cues and signals. Mehrabian found that the total impact of a message is

- 7% verbal (words only)
- 38% verbal (but including tone of voice, etc.)
- 55% non-verbal.

In short, we communicate far more non-verbally than verbally.

There now appears to be widespread agreement that the verbal channel is used mainly for conveying information and the non-verbal channel conveys interpersonal attitudes and emotions, which may or may not accord with the verbal message. Often our bodies transmit a very different message from our verbal message. As interviewers we must be aware of our own NV messages and those the people opposite us are sending.

The main elements of NVC are as follows:

Proximity

This refers to how close we get to other people or how close we allow others to get to us. Generally speaking, the closer the relationship the closer individuals get to one another. However, proximity is governed by cultural roles and so allowance should be made for this.

Research by Allan Pease indicated that there are four

Fig1.2 A comparison between Passive and Active Listening

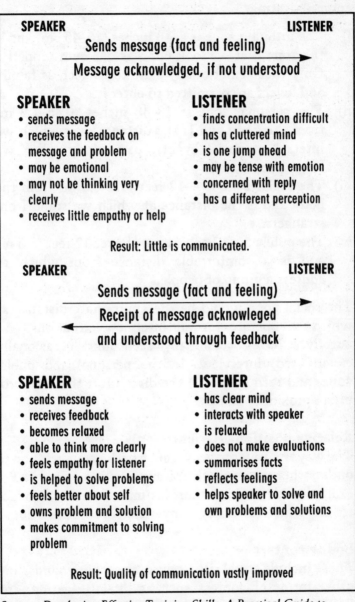

Source: *Developing Effective Training Skills: A Practical Guide to Designing and Delevering Group Training*, by Tony Pont. 2nd edition 1996, McGraw Hill, Maidenhead. Reproduced with permission of the publisher.

distinct zones that people usually maintain when communicating:

i)   The intimate zone is 6–18 inches (15–45 cm) and is the zone that we look upon as our own property. Only those emotionally close to us such as family and lovers are permitted to enter it.

ii)   The personal zone is 18–48 inches (0.45–1.2 m) from the body and is the distance over which we interact at social events, particularly when we know people well.

iii) The social zone is 4–12 feet (1.2–3.5 m) from the body and is the distance at which we stand from strangers.

iv)   The public zone has a range of over 12 feet (3.5 m) and is a comfortable distance from which to address a group of people.

The social zone would be the appropriate distance at which to operate for all interview situations. We ourselves have occasionally seen (and occasionally experienced) interviews in the personal and public zones and seen (and felt) the discomfort that inappropriate proximity causes.

Relative positions (Orientation)
The way two or more people are positioned in relation to one another can imply their frame of mind or intent. For example, side by side is more intimate/friendly than face to face, which can imply competition or confrontation.

Bodily contact
These include social rituals such as shaking hands, and other forms of contact such as hitting, kissing, etc. Bodily contact increases as relationships get closer but, as with proximity, different nationalities have different cultural norms.

Posture
Posture might indicate how tense or relaxed a person is. Leaning forward could imply enthusiasm or intimacy or aggression, while leaning back might indicate being relaxed or calm or disinterested. Leaning back with hands behind one's head can signify superiority and arrogance.

Gestures
For example:

Head – nodding, shaking, etc.
Hands – gesticulating and waving: fist or open hand.
Limbs – crossing the legs, folding the arms, opening the arms.

These gestures can indicate the person's frame of mind or reaction to events.

Facial expressions
The eyes: the degree of eye contact and type of gaze can express a range of emotions from interest to anger. Lack of eye contact might be due to shyness, lack of interest, or dishonesty. The position of the eyebrows can influence a person's expression. If raised, they may mean shock or interest, if lowered they may signal anger, depression, sadness.
The mouth: tight-lipped, smiling, or whatever – has a big impact on the facial expression.

The combination of all the facial features can signal a wide variety of emotions, but don't try to read too much into them – it is important to remember that expressions can easily be misinterpreted. The expression may even be fixed!

Appearance
Clothes, accessories, hairstyle and so on are, to an

extent, a statement about the person's values and project an image. It is important to dress appropriately and give a professional image.

When you are communicating, non-verbal signals are a source of information which should not be ignored, but equally they should not be given too much weight. All the factors should be assimilated together – no one aspect should be considered in isolation.

How do we use non-verbal communication?

Most of us consciously use non-verbal communication to support our verbal messages.

As a speaker we use NVCs to:

- emphasise meanings (gestures, facial expressions, etc.)
- encourage the listener to listen (eye contact, head and body movements, etc.)
- signal we are about to stop talking (raised eyebrows, head movements, etc.)

We also use NVCs consciously as a listener to:

- encourage the speaker to talk (nods, eye contact, tilting the head to one side, etc.)
- break into the conversation without actually inter-rupting (leaning forward, making a hand gesture, taking a deep breath through the mouth as if about to start talking, etc.)

We also observe the NVCs of the speaker to 'read' the underlying message, feelings, and so on. Whilst much of the non-verbal behaviour we exhibit is done consciously, some is spontaneous and unconscious. Perhaps these are the most telling 'signs' to watch for as an interviewer. Check whether the NVCs are congruent with the words that are being spoken – if not, probe for more information. An extreme example would be someone saying 'Yes' while shaking their head! Conflicting behaviours of this type happen more often than you would imagine.

Sometimes people use NVCs *in place of speaking*. For instance, you may have observed a reticent person in a committee meeting who, when asked for his/her views, 'pulls a face' in preference to actually talking. These signals provide an ideal opportunity to draw a person into the conversation. It would be foolish to assume that these 'signals' could be read accurately every time, so do ask for clarification: 'What do you mean by that', or, 'John, are you not happy with that?' or, 'What's the problem?'

Different NVCs communicate different messages. Below are a number of common behaviours. The column on the left encourages openness, trust and a relaxed but purposeful interaction; the column on the right encourages defensiveness, mistrust, anxiety and negative interactions. Be aware of their effects (particularly if you exhibit these) on others, and adopt the appropriate behaviours.

Do:	Don't:
Have an open posture	Cross your arms
Smile	Frown or scowl
Maintain eye contact; look at the person	Look away or stare at the person
Sit forward	Slouch in your chair; hide behind your desk; place your feet on desk or table
Display a relaxed appearance	Appear tense or nervous
Display open palms	Clench your fists; have your hands in your pockets; have your hands hidden; point with one finger

| Stay attentive and relatively still | Chew your pencil; fidget |
| Have legs uncrossed | Cross your legs |

Note the importance of the eyes and the hands in the messages we convey.

Concluding the interview

Experience or time constraints will indicate when the time has come to bring the interview towards its close. It is just as important to terminate the interview in a proper fashion as it is to start it. In short, endings are just as important as beginnings. They may be even more important because they represent the final impression and they could also represent the start of the next stage. There are no hard and fast rules as to how all types of interview should be concluded, but a number of guidelines apply:

- Invite questions or comments.
- Conclude on a positive note by stating what action will be taken. In the case of the Selection Interview this could be a follow-up letter in the following week; in the case of the Counselling Interview it could be contracting another appointment or series of appointments.
- Thank the interviewee for coming.

(f) Evaluation and follow-up

This stage, although short, is important and doesn't require a large commitment of time. By now, you should have formed your impressions and it is important that if you are to form a judgment it should be as free of bias as possible. There are a number of pitfalls in judging interviewees which we need to be aware of and avoid. These include:

i) *Halo effect*. This is where one feature positively influences our overall perception. Such features may be things such as the interviewee being tall or attractive or hailing from our own home area. Sometimes much deeper-seated psychological influences can influence us, such as seeing someone as a son/daughter figure who would benefit from our mentorship and tutelage.

ii) *Negative bias*. This is when we give a small amount of unfavourable information unnecesssary weight. For example, someone who worked for a company which made you redundant isn't therefore a bad worker.

iii) *Stereotypes*. With these we make assumptions on the basis of irrational and pre-conceived ideas. For example, someone whose eyebrows meet is untrustworthy; accountants are reticent; Americans are too brash.

iv) *Logical error*. This leads us to judge one trait by another that *seems* to be related. For example, someone with quick reactions may be judged as highly intelligent although speed of reaction is not an accurate gauge of intelligence.

v) *Error of leniency*. We are over-lenient because we are embarrassed to ask certain questions or disinclined to be harsh on the interviewee.

vi) *Prejudice*. We have certain values and beliefs which lead us to prejudge issues, positively or negatively, for example against a certain ethnic group.

vii) *Being judgmental*. Imposing our own views in sometimes inappropriate circumstances. This can happen in counselling.

There are two other aspects which you should also consider:

i) Checking that the proposed action has been taken and that the desired results have been actioned. Sometimes we may personally be involved with the follow-up: for example, contacting someone by telephone to make the offer of a job and informing them that the offer will shortly be confirmed in writing.

ii) Evaluating our own performance as an interviewer. This involves being totally honest with ourselves. It should be viewed as developmental, not purely critical. Every experience offers the opportunity to learn for those who want to take it. At its simplest, the evaluation could take the form of three questions.

- What did I do well?
- What did I do satisfactorily?
- What did I do poorly?

Whatever form of evaluation used, it is important, if we are to improve, to contract an action plan with ourselves and ruthlessly implement it. Remember, the skills of interviewing are valuable ones in a manager's armoury and can be used on numerous occasions, not only to enhance our own credibility, but to bring about improved performance in our work area.

Transactional Analysis – a model of interpersonal communication

A very useful model for understanding and improving interpersonal relations and communication is Transactional Analysis (or TA for short). TA was developed in the 1950s and 1960s by the Canadian psychotherapist, Eric Berne. It is a method used to analyse the basis from which another individual is communicating or interacting and thus decide how best to respond. It is a valuable tool that can be used in all life situations and the interview situation is no exception. Much distinctive jargon is associated with TA theory: 'complementary transactions', 'strokes', 'life scripts', 'tapes', 'games' and being 'OK' or 'not-OK'. Most of these will be briefly explained here, but readers who wish to learn more can consult the Further Reading section at the end of the book.

TA states that we communicate from three ego states. These are called Parent, Adult and Child (hence PAC), which are shown as three circles arranged vertically (see Figure 1.3) These three ego states together form our personality, which influences our behaviour. Since conception we are the sum of our experiences, ranging from childhood to adulthood and in most cases parenthood. All of us have had role models for these three stages. All collective experiences are stored in the brain and when we receive the appropriate stimulus they resurface as behaviour. The analogy is often made with a tape recorder – we record or store our life experiences and when the playback button is activated we replay the experience or recording.

We all operate from each of the three ego states and, according to TA theory, it is OK to adopt behaviour associated with any of the three stages if appropriate in the circumstances. Usually, though, and certainly in the interview situation, *it is best to function in the adult mode*.

Fig1.3 The three ego states used in Transactional Analysis: Parent, Adult, and Child

The ego states – basic structure

These represent the way we react to our external world. When we receive a stimulus, e.g. a question, a statement or a comment, we may react in a variety of ways – enthusiasm, eloquence, anger, anxiety, apprehension – and each reaction will reflect an underlying ego state. We may have been conditioned by our life experiences to react accordingly. The main ego states and their functions are described in Figure 1.4.

Fig1.4 The main functions of the TA ego states

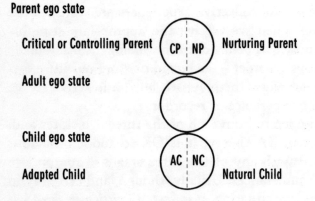

Parent ego state

This part of our personality is derived from the observation and imitation of, and the identification with our role models, particularly parents, in our childhood. We have learnt a set of attitudes, values and behaviours from our past role models and when we act in accordance with these we are acting from our parent ego state. Parents spend a great deal of time controlling and conditioning their children's behaviour, especially in the early years. They may also be very critical of their children's behaviour, seeking either to correct bad behaviour or control it. Some adopt a critical parent role with subordinates which often invites rebellion rather than obedience. Parents also spend a great deal of time nurturing or caring for their children. The need to both give and receive care and attention is present in all of us, irrespective of age. In some interviewing situations it is okay to adopt a caring parent approach, e.g. counselling.

Adult ego state

When we operate from this ego state we operate from the here and now. Objectivity, analysis, rationality, logic, detachment, lack of emotional involvement and impartiality are some of the words or phrases which characterise this ego state. It is this part of our personality that we use in effective information processing, problem solving and decision making. We need to display this part of our personality in a range of interviewing situations in the role of interviewer.

Child ego state

This is the part of our personality we largely learned in the early formative years up to the age of seven. It is divided into the Natural and Adapted Child functions. The former refers to our propensity to show our feelings in an uninhibited way, e.g. pleasure, and the latter refers to our ability to learn that certain behaviours in certain situations are inappropriate and our ability to adapt accordingly. In the latter we also learn that certain behaviours may gain parental approval or attention with a built in reward system, e.g. a bag of sweets. When the child part of our personality surfaces, e.g. by being spontaneous, self-centred, stubborn, attention seeking, by moaning, throwing tantrums and being self-indulgent, we are replaying behaviours, thinking and/or feelings that we experienced in our past and which often had a pay-off. These typical child-like behaviours can, and do, surface in adult behaviour patterns. As an interviewer we need to be aware of this part of human personality and how it may manifest itself with the interviewee in a range of interviewing situations. Good parenting practice should give us clues as to how best to deal with these behaviours, in addition to the practical advice offered later in this book.

TA and communication
Communication is a two-way process and nowhere is this more concentrated and evident than in the interview situation. An analysis of TA can be very helpful. If an individual speaks from the adult mode and is responded to as an adult, the communication is likely to be successful. This is called a *complementary* or *uncrossed transaction*. If, however, someone is speaking from the adult mode and the response is from the parent or child mode, then problems occur. This is called a *crossed transaction*.

Examples of uncrossed transaction are as follows:

Interviewer: How did you feel about taking the tests?
          (Adult.)
Interviewee: Good. I enjoyed it and I am interested to
          hear the results. (Adult.)

Another uncrossed transaction might be as follows:

Interviewer: You look a little puzzled. Shall I explain
          that last point again? (Parent to child.)
Interviewee: Gee, yes. I'll try and get it this time.
          (Child to parent.)

Diagrammatically the two are shown in Figure 1.5.
Examples of a crossed transaction are as follows:

Interviewer: I'd like to fix a time with you for your
          appraisal interview (Adult.)
Interviewee: Not again! I can't see the point, and
          besides I'm not ready. (Child to parent.)

Fig. 1.5: Uncrossed and crossed transactions are OK

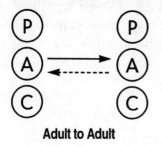

Adult to Adult

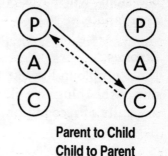

Parent to Child
Child to Parent

Another crossed transaction might be as follows:

Interviewer: You look a little puzzled. Shall I explain that last point again? (Adult.)

Interviewee: Well, if you understood it more yourself and could explain things clearly you wouldn't have to keep going over everything twice! (Parent to child.)

Diagrammatically the two are shown in Figure 1.6:

Fig. 1.6: Crossed transactions are not OK

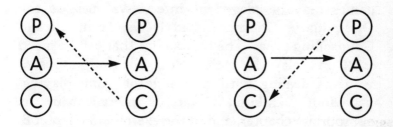

We can draw up a matrix to demonstrate the relationship between a range of communication skills and the three ego states. These are shown in Figure 1.7.

The matrix should reinforce the importance of

operating from the Adult mode, although there are occasions when the Nurturing Parent mode will be appropriate.

Strokes
Most people in life like to collect things. In TA terms, one of the things we like to do is 'collect stamps' which are units of recognition. Such units may be positive or negative.

(i) Positive strokes
This is positive feedback or 'warm fuzzies' and these recognise our contribution, make us feel valued and secure, and increase self-esteem and confidence. In short, they make people feel good about themselves. In the interview situation, such as Appraisal and Feedback (giving criticism), it is important to finish with a 'warm fuzzy'.

(ii) Negative strokes
This is negative feedback and is sometimes referred to as 'cold pricklies'. Some people collect these 'stamps' as part of a ritual of playing games such as in attention-seeking. The 'collector' or interviewee may well be operating from their Child ego state. Such games may be played at interviews such as the Disciplinary, Grievance, Bad News, Feedback and Counselling types. The best advice that can be given is, 'Don't play the game.' You will find suggested ways of dealing with the range of 'game-playing' behaviours exhibited at various interviews in the appropriate chapter, and in the exercise in chapter 8.

Summary

By following a systematic approach to interviewing, we can all become competent interviewers. Below is a

Fig. 1.7:

	Parent		Adult	Child
	Critical	Nurturing		
Voice	Condescending, criticising, patronising, accusing, putting down, raised voice.	Soft, gentle, concerned, reassuring.	Factual, calm, unemotional	Full of feeling, emotional
Words	This is a poor ... I wouldn't expect this from you! You must/will... This had better improve! I'm cross with you.	Are you feeling better? Is there anything I can do to help? How do you feel?	The 'six faithful serving men' (i.e. open questions). So, what you are saying is ...	I'm mad at you! Any words with a high feeling level.
Posture	Pompous, superior, on a pedestal, (behind the desk or feet on desk?). Tense, nervous, angry, staring.	Leaning towards the other person, arm around, protective.	Relaxed, but purposeful, eye-to-eye contact, open.	Self-conscious, looking away, playful, downbeat, slouching, hand in pockets.
Facial expression	Air of superiority, frowning, scowling, disapproving, aloof, tight-lipped.	Concerned, smiling, questioning.	Attentive, impassive, alert, occasional smile.	Surprise, downcast eyes, quivering lips, moist eyes or tears, gazing into space.
Gestures	Fingers pointing accusingly (telling), arms crossed, head shaking. Dismissive, back-of hand gestures, distant, air of superiority.	Quizzical expression, leaning towards the subject, possibly to embrace.	Open posture, leaning towards the other person to see and hear better, nodding encouragingly	Laughter, withdrawing or moving away, spontaneous responses, sighs of boredeom.
Feelings	Tied up with own agenda, other person has let them down, has compromised their standards, anger, irritation, reacts to provocation.	Tied up with the subject's agenda, protective, caring.	Controlled, calm, unemotional.	Tantrums, 'toy-throwing', sense of injustice, feels is the subject of unjust treatment. Calm, placid, compliant – trying to please parent.

checklist for interviewing which summarises the main points of this chapter. Good interviewers:

- set clear aims and objectives for the interview and clarify beforehand what information needs to be revealed
- keep their objectives clearly in their mind
- plan the interview but are prepared to be flexible
- engender a constructive climate by creating the right physical environment beforehand and taking time to establish rapport with the interviewee
- establish a pattern of questioning to follow; within this pattern they *do*:
  - ✓ use mainly open and probing questions
  - ✓ restrict the use of closed questions

  and *don't*:
  - ✗ interrupt
  - ✗ monopolise the conversation
  - ✗ answer the question for the interviewee
- use simple, clear, jargon-free language which is:
  - ✓ clear and specific
  - ✓ with questions pitched at the right level
  - ✓ logical
  - ✓ brief and conside wherever possible
- allow thinking time for response
- listen carefully and use the techniques of summarising and reflecting to clarify their understanding of the message
- analyse the interviewee's responses to get an overall impression (personality, communication skills, etc.) as well as focusing on specific information
- observe and interpret the interviewee's non-verbal messages (gestures, facial expressions, movements, etc.) which can reveal a great deal about the interviewee
- maintain an atmosphere of polite but purposeful

neutrality and are aware of their own non-verbal messages

- conclude on a positive note, take any questions, and summarise and explain what happens next
- in Transactional Analysis terms, communicate mainly from their Adult ego state
- *don't talk too much* (as a rough guide, aim for 20% talking and 80% listening).

This concludes the general information you'll need when conducting interviews. How to make these skills more interview-specific will be developed in the following chapters.

2

The Selection Interview

Selection Interviews are likely to be the interviews that most managers will have to conduct. Indeed, virtually every manager will be involved in a selection interview at some stage in their career, whether it be in the appointment of a young trainee or a senior executive. In some situations managers will conduct the interview on their own, whilst in other situations they may be part of a panel. The latter is particularly common in the UK in public sector appointments such as in the education profession.

The task of the interviewer(s) is to select a person who is likely to succeed in a certain job or range of jobs. Initially, therefore, some assessment will have to be made of job competence and 'fit'. The latter relates to such areas as relationship with others and company culture, which are nebulous terms but nonetheless reflect very real aspects. The interviewer has therefore to make a decision with some sort of predictive element of future success. Whilst job success can never be predicted with 100% accuracy, nevertheless, good preparation and interview techniques can greatly increase the chances of the correct choice being made in terms of job competency, general 'fit' and future success.

Two factors can help you to predict future success:

(i)   The biographical details of the candidate. In the

same way that some historians view the 'past as the key to the future', the selection interviewer can do the same. For example, individuals who have taken positions of influence and authority over others tend to seek similar positions in new situations.

(ii) Being very clear in your own mind what you are looking for. This will help you focus during the pre-interview and interview stages.

Pre-interview tasks

With all interactive situations the chances of success will be greatly increased with thorough preparation. As a general rule, preparation time to interview time should be in a ratio of 3:1, or at lowest 2:1. If you find this difficult to accept in terms of time and therefore cost, consider the cost of employing people, particularly the wrong ones. The cost of filling a vacancy can be an additional 25–33% above the normal salary. The return on investment of preparation time can therefore be considerable, especially if the right, rather than the wrong appointment is made.

The main tasks (not necessarily in order of importance) are:

(a) Draft/obtain a job description

The job description defines the main aspects of the job. In some situations, the job description may be a carbon copy of the job carried out by the previous holder, in which case the previous incumbent's job description is the starting point. A job description is an accurate description of the main duties and responsibilities of an individual job. It should clearly specify a number of Key Result Areas and the main lines of responsibility. In other situations, there may be no previous job description or the existing one will need amending to take account of changing circumstances. Whatever the situation, a job specification needs drafting at the advertising stage of the recruitment process.

The job specification can give the candidate a feel for the job and the opportunity to consider if a 'fit' exists. If the job has certain conditions attached to it which the interviewee will be unable to meet, then he/she can decide not to submit an application. For example, if the job requires mobility, non-drivers or disqualified drivers will be eliminated. Also, many people may find it difficult because of personal commitments to fulfil a job that requires a considerable time away from home. In short, a comprehensive job specification greatly reduces or eliminates a lot of uncertainty, confusion and time-wasting.

(b) Draft an employee specification or person profile

This will help you decide in advance what and who you are ideally looking for. It helps focus, and defines the employer's expectations. An employee specification describes the individual required in terms of skills (or competencies), qualifications and experience, and the personal attributes most suited to the job. There are several frameworks that can be used. The important thing is to use one that is appropriate for *you*, one that will help you conduct the selection procedure in an efficient and effective manner. Two examples are:

i) The Five-Point Plan (*J. Munro Fraser*)
> *Impact on others*
> *Qualifications*
> *Innate abilities*
> *Motivation*
> *Adjustment*

ii) The Seven-Point Plan (*Alec Rodger*)

Physical makeup. This includes such aspects as sex, age, health, physique, injuries, medical treatments, etc.

General or specific intelligence. Includes general ability such as verbal, numerical, spatial skills; critical reasoning skills; analytical skills; creative skills, etc. The ones most appropriate to the job can be targeted. If ability in one or more is crucial to job success, then these can be tested by a range of psychometric tests.

Educational attainments. This includes degrees, diplomas, certificates, professional qualifications, in-service education, etc.

Special aptitudes. This could include such aspects as verbal and numerical skills, mechanical skills, linguistic skills. One or more may be very important for job success.

Personal disposition. This relates to a number of personality traits relating to the kind of work to be done and the team with which the candidate will be working. Does the job require long hours of working solo or is teamworking vitally important? Is the person a leader or follower or maverick? Must the individual be able to cope with high stress levels? If one or more traits are vital to job success, appropriate psychometric tests can be used.

Interests. What sort of spare-time interests would be useful? Intellectual or practical? Solitary or social? Physical or sedentary? These also give clues about personality. Does the candidate have membership of a professional organisation that would be useful?

Personal circumstances. Are there any circumstances which would negatively affect the person's ability to do the job?

Whatever the headings decided, it is usually helpful to subdivide each of the relevant headings into two sections, namely ESSENTIAL and DESIRABLE. This can be of great help both in drawing up the person specification and in shortlisting. Using such headings to shortlist, on the basis of an objective assessment, also demonstrates objective and unbiased shortlisting and helps go some way to meet the Equal Opportunities legislation that may currently be in force. The legal requirements of Equal Opportunities legislation are beyond the scope of this book, but *all* managers are advised to ensure that they comply, and if in doubt, consult those who know – often the Personnel or Human Resources Department of the organisation.

Using a Seven-Point Plan very similar to that of Rodger's, an outline employee specification might look something like Figure 2.1.

(c) Ensure you comply with existing legislation

In recent years increasing emphasis has been given to Equal Opportunities to avoid discrimination against certain groups of people. The law in this area is constantly changing. If you are uncertain check with your organisation's Human Resources Department, or legal staff, or seek outside advice.

(d) Process the applications

Once you have the applications in, it is important to process them correctly. According to your organisation's procedure, the applications may either be on a standard application form or by the submission of a CV. Whatever the format, the interviewer(s) should carry out the following:

Fig. 2.1

Employee Specification Form

The purpose of this document is to enable you to draw up a specification of the type of person who is exactly appropriate for the job to be filled. It is a valuable aid to successful recruitment.

Against each of the major headings you are asked to record 'essential' and 'desirable' requirements.

Requirements	Essential	Desirable
PHYSICAL MAKE-UP Consider important aspects such as sex, age, health and physique, dress, bearing and speech, and then write a statement of your requirements.		
INTELLIGENCE Consider the mental content of the work and whether or not it calls for special abilities, e.g. verbal, numerical or spatial.		
EDUCATION AND TRAINING Consider the extent of education and training necessary: school, university, other full-time education, part-time education and professional training. State certificates and/or degrees necessary, listing sujects where appropriate.		

Fig 2.1 continued

Requirements	Essential	Desirable
JOB EXPERIENCE Consider experience necessary (in the light of any job training the Company will provide): jobs held, in what industries and what size of company, supervising experience, salary and promotion progression. Give the minimum length of experience.		
DISPOSITION Consider personality and character traits, bearing in mind the nature of the work and the working group, e.g. what degree of autonomy: will person be closely supervised or have to influence others? What stresses must he/she be able to withstand?		
INTERESTS AND ACTIVITIES Consider what sort of spare-time interests would be useful or desirable, e.g. social, intellectual, physical. Of what professional societies, clubs, etc., would membership be useful?		

Fig 2.1 continued

Requirements	Essential	Desirable
CIRCUMSTANCES Consider home circumstances, marital status, etc., in relation to whether or not the job involves travelling, moving home, shift-work, etc.		

(i)   Draw up a shortlist.
(ii) Invite the candidates for interview. This is usually done by letter and usually the candidates are given adequate notice in order to make the necessary personal and work arrangements.
(iii) Go through the submitted applications or CVs and highlight areas that will need clarification. Points that arise from this inspection of the CVs can be noted on the interview plan.

In the following exercise, we give an example of a CV that has a number of omissions. Please note that the CV bears no resemblance to any person, place, organisation or potential job. It is merely intended as an exercise to show how careful reading can highlight areas to probe with skilful questioning.

Exercise 1

Figure 2.2 is an example of a curriculum vitae. If you decided to shortlist Mr Brown, there would be a number of points requiring clarification at interview. Examine the CV and list the areas you should investigate. Then read the points we have noted, below.

Fig. 2.2

Curriculum Vitae

	Joseph Sidney Brown
Address:	28 Cornwall Avenue, Dunston,
	New Town, Southamptonshire
Telephone:	New Town 234234
Marital Status:	Married (3 dependants)
Age:	34 years
Health:	Good
Education:	Frederick Jones Comprehensive School,
	New Town, 1973–78
Qualifications:	GCSE – 5 subjects
	Associate Member of Institute of Personnel and Development
	Certificate in Training & Development
	IPD (Institute of Personnel Development) – Stage I

Employment History:

Dec 1993–date	Personnel Manager to W. J. Kinder (Packaging) Ltd. Responsible for all personnel matters for 750 employees, including selection and recruitment, wages/salary, administration, industrial relations.
Jan 1993–Sept 1993	Personnel Officer with J.K. Developments Ltd. Responsible for all personnel matters for 350 employees.
Oct 1987–Dec 1992	Training Adviser with Hotel & Catering Industries Training Board. Responsible for training advice to companies in the Board's East Midlands Region.
Sept 1980–Sept 1987	Training Administrator with Southamptonshire College of Further Education. General administration for training courses across the College.
Dec 1978–July 1980	Office Assistant – Southamptonshire *Daily Bugle*.
Hobbies:	Bob sleighing, travel, reading, DIY.

Points to probe at interview

i)   Brown has not been very specific regarding his dependants. You should probe this area.

ii)   He has entered the word 'date' in connection with his last or current job. It is not clear whether Brown has left the company. If he has quit the job then his reason(s) for going must be examined, as (we assume) there was no alternative employment on offer. Was he sacked?

iii) Most of the job responsibilities of Brown's employment are poorly described. This needs detailed investigation.

iv)   There is a gap of several weeks between Brown's last and penultimate jobs. Why?

v)   Details of his educational qualifications are vague. What subjects did he pass at GCSE? Where did he obtain the other qualifications? What level of success did he achieve?

vi)   Bob sleighing? An interesting hobby! Look at the remaining hobbies with a suspicious eye.

vii) Does Brown have a car licence? This is important in a job requiring mobility.

viii) What are Brown's current salary level and salary expectations?

(e) Make all the necessary arrangements

This refers to location, room layout, conditions, and so on, which were outlined in chapter 1. In short, ensure that you create the appropriate environmental conditions to ensure a successful and effective interview.

Now that you have completed all your preparations you are ready to meet your interviewee(s).

Conducting the interview

First impressions are crucial. You should therefore strive to do all within your power to ensure that the candidate's first impressions both of the organisation and of you yourself are as favourable as they can be. Remember, as interviewer, you are a representative of the organisation and should therefore strive to give a professional impression. There is no need to go overboard, but a courteous welcome and a cup of tea or coffee is always appreciated (particularly after a long journey) and costs very little. Doubtless many readers can recall numerous instances of abrupt and discourteous welcomes as they arrived, with some trepidation, for an interview.

At the interview itself, a number of preliminaries are necessary. These will include introductions, outline of the interview and how the interview will be conducted. There may be a casual conversation relating to topics unrelated to the job, merely as a means of helping the interviewee relax and overcome nerves. Good interviewers will progress smoothly into the questioning phase with the interviewee hardly realising the interview has begun, by starting with 'safe' or non-challenging questions first before moving on to other areas that will make greater demands upon the interviewee.

As an interviewer you will have to probe for information relating to experience, qualifications, ambitions and personal circumstances. At the same time as you are getting factual information about these areas, the responses will be giving you clues about personality, temperament, attitude, and so on, plus a feel for how the person will fit into the team or department as well as the culture of the organisation. An element of deciding on this 'fit' will partly depend on intuition or 'gut feel', but experienced interviewers, if they have elicited the right information by skilful questioning, will have a sound factual base to back up their intuitive judgments.

A key skill in good selection interviewing technique is to ensure that the interview is not and should not appear to be, an interrogation. An 'aggressive grilling' is not a positive experience and achieves nothing. Rather, it should be conducted as a purposeful and steered conversation, with the aim of establishing conditions in which the candidate will reveal accurate and comprehensive factual information about him or herself. Another important skill is to control the interview in such a way as to ensure that irrelevancies are kept to a minimum and information emerges as quickly as possible. The key to achieving these objectives is the use, throughout the interview, of open (particularly probing) questions. The interviewer who employs this type of questioning will find that the level of effort required – particularly in terms of time spent speaking and mental planning – will be greatly reduced. The interviewee will have to respond with carefully considered and revealing answers so that he/she will be doing most of the hard work, whilst the interviewer considers and assesses the replies.

Open questions were outlined in chapter 1 (see pages 20–22) and are quite simply questions that cannot be answered by a 'yes' or a 'no'. Here are some examples of open questions in the selection interview context:

What   What did you do then ... ?

What were your responsibilities ... ?

What happened then ... ?

What subjects did you take ... ?

What did you prefer ... ?

What sort of ... ?

What did you learn about yourself from ... ?

When   When was that ... ?

When did that happen ... ?

When did you go ... ¿

When did you decide ... ¿

When did the company ... ¿

When will you know ... ¿

Why   Why was that ... ¿

Why did you choose... ¿

Why do you think that ... ¿

Why did you do ... ¿

Why did they ... ¿

Why do you feel ... ¿

Why did you say that ... ¿

Where   Where was that ... ¿

Where did you go next ... ¿

Where were you when ... ¿

Where did you do ... ¿

Where do you think ... ¿

Where will you be ... ¿

Where do you see yourself in 5 years ... ¿

Which   Which do you prefer ... ¿

Which course did you ... ¿

Which were your best ... ¿

Which department was ... ¿

Which was that ... ¿

Which way do you ...¿

Who   Who did you work with ... ¿

Who was at ... ¿

Who suggested ... ¿

Who went to ... ¿

Who influenced you ... ¿

Who will you involve ... ¿

How   How did that come about ... ¿

How do you think that ... ¿

How much did that ... ¿

How did you get ... ¿

How was that ... ¿

How do you feel about ... ¿

Other ways of phrasing open questions include:

> Tell me about ...
> Please describe ...
> Could you elaborate on ... ?
> And then ... ?

The manner in which open-ended questions are asked will determine whether the interview is an interrogation or, as should be the case, a steered and friendly discussion. The interviewer should display a marked interest in the candidate and, although there is an overall need for the conversation to be firmly controlled by the interviewer, the candidate should feel that he or she is being treated with a degree of respect and importance.

As interviewer, you must guard against the interview going off at a tangent and losing control of it. Side issues and points of interest must be probed, but the interviewer should always be in command of the situation; you should steer the discussion towards achieving your objectives. Remember that, unlike oral presentations where you are in control by talking for 100% of the time, with an interview you are in control by talking for up to only 20% of the time. Any adjustments to the tiller should therefore be focused, meaningful and objective.

The skill of asking the right questions, i.e. those that will yield profitable answers, requires some training effort and experience, but, like all social skills, this can be obtained through practice. Practice makes perfect and once the skill has been internalised (when you have reached the stage of unconscious competence), you will ask open questions without thinking and in a variety of situations outside the interview. To help you get into the habit of asking open questions, here is another exercise to complete.

Exercise 2

Here is a list of twenty questions, all relating to information you might wish to obtain at interview. But, it is not just *what* you ask, but *how* you ask, that will determine your effectiveness as an interviewer. The column on the left is how *not* to phrase your questions; the column on the right suggests an alternative phrasing. Complete the exercise by covering up the right-hand column and then compare your suggestion with ours. Some of your suggestions for the right-hand column may be better than ours.

Sample open-ended questions

Please remember that these are sample questions and may or may not be relevant to any given interview.

Don't use	Do use
1 Did you enjoy your last job?	1 Tell me what you enjoyed about your last job.
2 Do you feel you learned a lot while you were in school?	2 What things, related to this job, do you feel you learned most about in school?
3 Were you attracted to seek work here because of the salary being offered?	3 Tell me, what was it that attracted you to seek work in our organisation?
4 Do you feel you are qualified for this job?	4 Would you describe why you feel you are qualified for this job?
5 Wouldn't you say that you've changed jobs rather often?	5 How do you feel about the frequency with which you've changed jobs?

6 Have you ever been required to demonstrate leadership?

6 In what ways have you been required to demonstrate leadership in the past?

7 Wouldn't it have been better just to admit you made a mistake?

7 Given the opportunity, what would you have done differently?

8 Have you found that people often react that way to you?

8 Why did you feel people reacted in that way?

9 Have you ever had personality clashes with any other people in that company?

9 How did you feel about the people you worked with, all things considered?

10 A great deal of that kind of work has to be done on this job, and I get the impression you don't enjoy doing it.

10 Was there anything about that kind of work you didn't like?

11 I suppose you left that department because there was little or no opportunity for advancement.

11 Why did you decide to transfer to a different department?

12 Were you ever asked to make decisions?

12 What kind of decisions did you regularly make on this job?

13 Were you closely supervised on your last job?

13 How much contact did you have with your boss on a day-to-day basis?

14 Naturally, we want someone to stay with our company for a number of years – do you anticipate you would be able to do that?

14 What are you looking for in a job change at this time?

15 I've heard that was a terrible company to work for – do you agree?

15 Was there anything about the company that you didn't particularly like or disagreed with?

16 We need someone who can really solve problems in this department – have you ever done that before?

16 Could you describe some particularly tough problems you have had to deal with?

17 We need someone who can handle a lot of pressure – do you have the ability to do that?

17 Would you describe the kind of responsibilities you've been asked to assume in the past?

18 In your last job, were you responsible for cash transactions, or was that your assistant's responsibility, and what was the system for balancing and checking the cash account?

18 In your last job, who was responsible for checking the cash transactions? And what was the system for balancing and checking the cash account?

19 The successful applicant for this post will be required to control the staff with a firm hand – would you be capable of this?

19 How do you feel about managing the department in which close controls are necessary?

20 Do you have any hobbies?

20 What do you do in your spare time?

Towards the end of the interview, the interviewer must ensure that the interview is closed in a professional manner. Also, towards the end, the interviewer may do the majority of the talking because the following tasks need to be accomplished:

i) Invite questions from the interviewee, particularly about the job prospects and the organisation.

ii) Inform the interviewee of what action will be taken after the interview, e.g. letter of rejection or offer, a second interview. With regard to the latter, you should do very little different from the first interview in terms of preparation and conduct. You may decide to involve a superior in order to verify your decision and to cover yourself. This is fine provided a decision is made and the interviewee is not asked back for several more interviews. (It does happen!) Continual dithering and prevarication with regard to a decision gives off negative messages about the organisation so that the candidate may decide to go elsewhere.

iii) Deal with issues relating to expenses.

iv) Thank the interviewee for coming. Even if you have decided that there is no chance of a job being offered, common courtesies should be observed to maintain your own and the organisation's professional image. In the situation where the interviewer intends to offer the job to the interviewee, it is important that the benefits of joining the organisation are sold. Hopefully, this will be reinforcing the professional image given by the competent interviewer! There is no doubt that incompetent interviewing repels and good interviewing can attract candidates. As part of the sales pitch this might be the time to give out relevant company literature.

After the interview

Immediately after the interview is the time to assess the interviewee's suitability for the position based upon:

- your subjective impressions of the candidate which include impressions, 'gut feel', etc.
- any objective data from testing, if administered
- references (if available)
- your own objective analysis of the candidate. It might be helpful to you (particularly if you are relatively inexperienced) to use a Candidate Assessment form similar to the one outlined below, which is based around the Seven-Point Plan described earlier. Whilst it is somewhat specialised, it can be useful in helping you verify your own subjective impressions and, more importantly, come to a decision. Making and owning the final decision can be a painful process, but eventually one will have to be made. Whilst there is no guarantee that you will get it right every time, if you have conducted an effective interview in order to get the relevant information, the chances of making the right appointment are greatly increased.

Fig. 2.3

CONFIDENTIAL

Candidate assessment form

Name   Job

Interviewer   Date

This assessment form has been so designed that you can record your impressions of a candidate's suitability for employment against the standards defined in the Employee Specification Form for the post to be filled. Each major area should be assessed and rated on the following scale:

OQ – Over-qualified   WQ – Well qualified

AQ – Adequately qualified   NQ – Not qualified

Under the heading *Overall comment*, write a statement of your findings about the candidate, giving your prediction for his/her future should he/she be offered a post in the Company.

Indicate your findings by ringing the appropriate gradings.

Requirement	Notes	Rating
PHYSICAL MAKEUP Consider age, health, appearance, bearing, speech and dress.		OQ WQ AQ BQ NQ
INTELLIGENCE How does candidate deal with questions? What evidence is there of effective use of intelligence? Does he/she have any special ability?		OQ WQ AQ BQ NQ
EDUCATION AND TRAINING Consider the extent and quality of candidate's education and training. What part has he/she played in non-academic life at school/university? What were his/her best/worst subjects, etc.?		OQ WQ AQ BQ NQ
JOB EXPERIENCE Has candidate made progress in his/her chosen field? What are his/her strengths/weaknesses? Has he/she held responsible supervisory posts? What is his/her own objective? What are candidate's relationships with his/her own boss?		OQ WQ AQ BQ NQ

Fig. 2.3 continued

Requirement	Notes	Rating
DISPOSITION Consider candidate's maturity vs. immaturity; confidence, reliability; extrovert vs. introvert, reaction to stress, etc.		OQ WQ AQ BQ NQ
INTERESTS AND ACTIVITIES Consider the range and depth of interests and activities and their relationship to the job to be filled.		OQ WQ AQ BQ NQ
CIRCUMSTANCES What are candidate's exact domestic circumstances?		OQ WQ AQ BQ NQ
MOTIVATION Consider whether or not candidate is realistic about his/her own ability and in which types of situation he/she would react favourably/unfavourably.		OQ WQ AQ BQ NQ
OVERALL COMMENT Based on all available facts, what is your impression of the candidate? Could he/she do the job under consideration; and what is your estimate of his/her potential?		OQ WQ AQ BQ NQ

RECOMMENDATION
e.g. Do not engage
     Shortlist
     Offer appointment
     Consider for ... Etc.		

Post-interview follow-up

Depending upon the final decision, a number of tasks need to be carried out:

- If rejected, the candidate needs to be politely informed. This is usually done by letter.
- If not rejected, the candidate needs to be invited back for a subsequent interview of contacted to be offered the job. This is usually done by phone and/or letter.
- References and a medical report may need to be obtained, and/or evidence of educational qualifications. The job offer may be conditional upon these being satisfactory.
- A contract of employment and relevant details of the package issued.

Summary

Selection interviews are the ones that most managers are likely to be involved in. Whilst every candidate, and therefore interview, is different, there are a number of common tasks which should be carried out in order to conduct an effective interview and to increase the chances of making the right choice. These are:

- thorough preparation *before* the interview, carrying out all the required tasks
- ensuring you have a clear job description of the vacant post
- having a good idea of the kind of person you are seeking
- using the interview to obtain the information you seek by using the appropriate questioning and listening techniques: open questions and summarising are the two most useful skills
- using all the information to reach a decision, which should be quickly and courteously communicated to the candidate
- honestly evaluating your own performance and using every interview as a benchmark for future improvement.

The Appraisal Interview

Many organisations now have some form of annual appraisal of their employees. In the UK, with over 12,000 organisations registering to achieve the Investors in People (IIP) standard in the period 1991–97, the number of organisations that have an appraisal scheme has increased dramatically, and whereas in the past appraisal was confined to large organisations, it has now become widely adopted by small and medium enterprises (SMEs). Whilst the appraisal process should be an end in itself, in some organisations it does have varying degrees of influence on pay and promotion issues.

What, then, is appraisal? It is a systematic way of helping the organisation to make the most of the capabilities of their employees and help them realise their potential. In short, if applied effectively, it is a very valuable management and organisational development tool.

Most appraisal interviews are conducted annually, although there may be mini-reviews conducted at varying intervals, e.g. every three months during the twelve-month period. The appraisal interview is a scheduled meeting between manager and subordinate with the following objectives:

- to discuss the subordinate's progress and achievements, priorities and problems during the previous year

- to set objectives for the year ahead, which should involve setting targets linked to the Key Result Areas (KRAs) of the job (see Appendix I)
- to discuss the subordinate's future potential and career development, and immediate training needs.

The appraisal interview is NOT the following:

- an opportunity to give the appraisee his or her school report, full of 'could do better', 'tries hard', 'needs to concentrate more', and so on
- a secret report on the subordinate which is placed on record without the subordinate ever seeing it
- an opportunity for the manager to 'spell out progress' by adopting a 'telling' mode
- an opportunity, using rank, to browbeat an employee with your views of their failings and weaknesses
- a Disciplinary Interview relating to situations during the previous twelve months; these should have been dealt with at the time of occurrence
- an attack on the appraisee's personality
- a salary discussion.

The main reason why appraisal fails is not the appraisal system itself, but the inability of managers to conduct the interview properly. In some instances the interview is so poorly conducted that it would have been better if it had never been staged.

Benefits of appraisal

If the interview is conducted properly, there are three main beneficiaries:

(a) The individual

Most employees are egocentric when it comes to their job. They are interested in their job and most take pride in their work. They like feedback on performance, either recognition for a job well done or constructive feedback and support to do it better. They don't like being demeaned and ridiculed. They also welcome the opportunity to discuss their future in the organisation and future career possibilities.

(b) The manager

Any process that opens up the communication channels between two people must be good. An open, honest discussion should improve working relationships, individual productivity and effectiveness. Carrying out appraisal interviews is very developmental for the manager, giving practice in a range of interpersonal skills that can be applied in other situations. It also helps managers keep their 'fingers on the pulse' so that they are aware of what is going on in their work area.

(c) The organisation

An opening up of the communication channels throughout the organisation should significantly improve working relationships. It can highlight priorities, identify future training needs and ensure that they are fully in line with the Business Plan so that training not only increases individual effectiveness but should make a significant contribution to the bottom line.

In terms of planning succession in the company's various positions, it helps the organisation take a more strategic view by identifying people with potential and ensuring that training provision is geared not only to short-term goals but to long-term ones as well. It is much more economical to develop your own talent than to buy in from outside.

Before the interview

Unlike Counselling and Grievance Interviews (chapters 4 and 7), the appraisal interview requires a great deal of preparation beforehand. It probably requires *more preparation than any other interview* and there is, or should be, a wealth of information to consult. Managers who think they will be able to 'think on their feet', 'go with the flow' or that 'it will all come out in the wash' will almost certainly be involved in a disaster. Not only does the appraisee suffer, but a slipshod approach gives off a poor message about the appraiser as a manager and the attitude of the organisation to its employees. In the eyes of the appraisee, it is a very important day, and it should be treated as such by the appraiser too.

The appraisal interview is a *two-way process* between manager and subordinate. No one is better placed to discuss the subordinate's work. The direct-line or reporting relationship is often not present in other types of interview; for example, the Exit and Selection Interviews may be conducted by a representative from Human Resources, and Disciplinary Interviews may be conducted by a senior manager.

The following need to be prepared:

(a) Physical setting

- The room should be private, free from interruptions.
- Aim for a furniture arrangement that is conducive to informality and informal dialogue (see pages 10–11).

(b) Timing

- Allow plenty of time for the interview.
- Allow plenty of time between interviews. Don't arrange more than two a day because appraisal interviews are demanding and sap energy. Otherwise

'tail-end Tina' at 4.45 pm is likely to get a raw deal.

(c) With regard to the appraisee

- Give the appraisee adequate notice: ten to fourteen days is probably appropriate. It is advisable that you arrange the interview *yourself* rather than get a secretary or someone else to arrange it. This is because the personal touch is usually well received and gives the appraisee the correct impression that the forthcoming interview is important and not something that has to be got out of the way. More importantly, you can brief the appraisee on areas that you wish to discuss so that he or she comes fully prepared to discuss the important and relevant areas. The appraisee has no excuses for not preparing but also is not caught unprepared, which is not the way to conduct an appraisal interview.
- If the organisation has a pre-appraisal form (and many do), issue it, with a clear briefing.
- Consider the individual and his or her likely response to criticism, praise and feedback. Be aware of any particular issues that are likely to figure high on his or agenda, and your likely response.
- Have a quiet word with others with whom the appraisee works. This is not for subversive reasons, but rather there may be a problem in the appraisee's work area which will need discussing in the appraisal interview.

(d) Documentation

The following need to be read and digested before the interview:

- the appraisee's personal file
- the appraisee's job description, which must be up-to-date and should clearly state the Key Result Areas of the job

• the previous appraisal form, which should contain information relating to objectives or targets, and standards of performance. Performance against these will form the basis of an objective appraisal.

(e) The interview structure

Prepare an outline structure with particular emphasis on the beginning. Usually if you get on track at the start the rest tends to follow on more smoothly. Have a number of questions written down, especially for tricky areas, but, of course, be prepared to be flexible. It is easier to 'go with the flow' from a thoroughly prepared base. You should aim to get the appraisee to do most of the talking.

(f) Yourself

Having prepared all the factors outlined above, give youself a few minutes prior to the interview to gather your thoughts and stay calm. You could be nervous too, but thorough preparation should help allay any fears. Also, be aware of any 'emotional luggage' that you may bring to the interview and take the necessary steps to park it. For example, if you arrive at the interview straight from a blazing argument with spouse, teenagers, or work colleagues, you may not be in a fit state to conduct a rational, calm and objective discussion. We tend to project our anxieties, frustrations, and so on, onto others, which can significantly impact upon the effectiveness and outcome of the interview.

During the interview

You are now calm, focused and relaxed. You have thoroughly prepared, so have considerably increased your chances of success. You have an outline structure, a carefully worded opening and a number of relevant and correctly phrased questions. It is time to begin. Welcome the appraisee and get down to business straight away. It is advisable to re-state the purpose of the interview and to explain how you intend to proceed. A good, confident, purposeful and focused start is crucial – it helps relax both interviewer and interviewee and gives you both confidence. As you will probably be taking notes, explain what will happen to these notes after the interview.

As you may be encountering a range of defensive behaviours from the appraisee, ranging from nervousness to aggression, you need to proceed accordingly. Likely reactions should have been anticipated during the preparation, which will have influenced your approach and the order of play. It is important to try and eliminate both our own and others' defensive behaviours, as they can get in the way of open and honest communication.

Having dealt with the introduction to the whole interview, the interviewer needs to focus on the following:

- the previous year
- the year ahead
- the appraisee's future career and development.

Like the whole interview itself, each one of these segments will have a beginning, a middle and an end.

The previous year

This discussion is a review of performance and should focus on the key areas of the job, addressing targets, objectives, priorities, strengths and weaknesses for each key area.

How you approach this is vitally important and the following approach is suggested:

- Focus on the individual's performance and not the individual as a person. Reference, therefore, should always be made to *what* the individual has done or said and the interviewer must be in a position to support any statements made with *factual* evidence.

- Avoid, if possible, the 'telling' mode. Instead, get opinions and assessments from the *appraisee*, by asking open questions. For example:

  'Tell me about the XYZ project. What difficulties did you encounter?'
  'What successes did you have?'
  'How successful do you think you were?'
  'What problems did you encounter?'
  'What did you do well?'
  'What did you do badly?'
  'If we could turn the clock back twelve months, what would you do differently?'
  'What have you learnt from this project?'
  'What would be your overall assessment of the way you carried out your tasks in relation to the project?'
  And so on, using whatever is appropriate.

  These open and probing questions should be supported by the techniques of summarising and reflecting.

Why do we *ask* for performance evaluations before going into a telling mode and giving feedback? Quite simply, if there is a performance problem, individuals are usually aware of it and will frequently be self-critical – they are often more critical of themselves than the manager would have been. By allowing the appraisee to identify the shortfall, rather than having it pointed out to them (especially if it is pointed out personally and aggressively), a whole range of defensive behaviours is avoided.

Also, by asking, you may be made aware of problems or issues that you were previously unaware of, which adversely affected performance. Corrective action may be within your power, especially if you are part of the problem!

If the appraisee has been over-critical of him or herself, you can correct it. If they have not been sufficiently critical then you will have to give your feedback, making sure that all statements are supported by factual evidence. And, if the appraisee has not been sufficiently generous in praising his or her own efforts, then again you can offer praise. Whatever the evaluation, always try to finish on a positive note.

When all matters have been discussed relating to the previous year, the content of the discussion needs to be summarised and recorded. This is particularly important if a number of action points emerge from the appraisal. It will be most meaningful, again, if the *appraisee* summarises the discussion and action points and the interviewer records them.

The year ahead

This is the next major stage of the interview and you should aim for a smooth transition from the previous stage. Something like, 'OK, John, we seem to have fully discussed last year. Let's move on to look at the next twelve months.'

What emphasis you give this part of the discussion will be greatly influenced by what has gone before. With a poor appraisal, the focus needs to be on how to achieve the required improvements in performance. With a good appraisal, the focus needs to be on a more productive use of the appraisee's talents and strengths, and the setting of objectives or targets that will be more stretching. The year ahead may offer the challenge of new projects which will make demands on skills and competencies not yet required or revealed. As with the discussion on the previous year, *ask* for suggestions and go for joint agreement. Appraisee suggestions increase ownership and commitment. In order to meet the challenges of the year ahead the appraisee may need extra support and/or training from the organisation. Whatever is agreed, the discussion needs summarising and recording.

Future development

This stage of the interview should be marked by the same seamless transition as before and the same structure as before. *Ask* about their future plans, ambitions and aspirations. You may or may not agree with their own assessment of future potential, but it does provide a valuable opportunity to obtain insight into what they are thinking. If they are high-potential, you can confirm this, but do be aware of making any promises or guarantees that you can't fulfil. It may, of course, be the start of future progression for the appraisee because their immediate manager is the first point of contact to reach the organisation's promotion network.

Concluding the interview

Good endings are as important as good beginnings so it is important to finish on a harmonious and positive note. The following needs to be done:

- all the main points of the discussion, and particularly action points, need summarising
- give the appraisee the opportunity to add to what has been said or to ask anything
- give praise for what has been done well
- state what is to happen to the interview notes
- thank the appraisee for their contribution in the last year
- finish on an upbeat note about the year ahead.

After the interview

A cup of coffee is probably the first task, after which the following should be done:

- The interview details are recorded *immediately* after the event, whilst it is still fresh in the mind of the appraiser. This reduces the chances of any decisions or agreements being overlooked or forgotten. The completed record of the interview will, of course, provide the starting point in preparation for next year's appraisal interview.
- The completed report is usually sent to the appraiser's superior for comment and then to the appraisee who is usually asked to record their views and sign it. The completed record of the interview should hold *no* surprises for the appraisee if everything was correctly summarised.
- A copy is usually sent to the organisation's central coordinator for appraisals, which is usually the Human Resources Department. This will provide them with useful information in planning training provision for the year ahead, as well as providing information relating to future salary reviews, manpower and succession planning. The Human Resources Department can also evaluate whether all parts of the organisation are contributing fully to the organisation's business plan.
- Keep a copy for your own records and to enable you periodically to monitor the implementation of action plans.
- Provide feedback to the Human Resources Department on the effectiveness of the appraisal procedure, especially documentation. The feedback and any suggestions can be evaluated with a view to future improvement. Appraisal is a valuable organisational development tool so improvements to the process benefit the organisation.

Summary

The main points of this chapter are:

- Appraisals are becoming more widespread as organisations recognise the importance of developing their most important resource.
- However good the appraisal system, it is only as good as the people who implement it. The main reason most appraisal systems fail is because managers cannot interview.
- Appraisal interviews are usually held annually and focus on: discussion of the previous year's performance; setting objectives or targets for the year ahead; and discussion of the appraisee's future development.
- Appraisal interviews require a great deal of preparation beforehand by the appraiser, who is almost always the appraisee's line manager. A range of documentary evidence needs to be consulted, including the job description and last year's appraisal form.
- At interview the appraiser should:
  - focus on facts and behaviours, not personalities
  - use open and probing questions and largely avoid 'telling'. *Questions, not comments*.
  - listen carefully, summarise and reflect regularly
  - record proceedings, particularly action points
  - end on a positive note.
- After the interview the proceedings should be written up immediately and the appraisee should be asked to sign the report as a true record of the interview. The appraiser and the central coordinator should keep a copy.

Note: a brief description of some of the terms used in this chapter relating to the job itself are briefly described in Appendix I at the end of the book.

The Counselling Interview

Is there a place for counselling in the workplace?

We certainly need to recognise that as the rate of change increases and the more complex and fast-moving life becomes, so personal problems increase and therefore the greater the need for skills, support systems and counselling in order to find solutions. Organisations often accept, and sometimes even encourage, the workforce to take problems from work home with them in order to find solutions that cannot be found in the working day. In the same way, people carry their personal problems from home with them wherever they go. Problems from home are never confined there and always find their way into the workplace to some degree. In chapter 1, the Counselling Interview was defined as a means of 'helping the interviewee to identify and solve their own problems, which could be either work related or personal'. Whilst this can happen in a formal counselling interview, counselling can also take place in a very unstructured and informal way when an individual pours out their problem, e.g. over a cup of coffee in the canteen. In this situation, the counsellor may just be a sympathetic pair of ears.

Anyone can counsel, but not all managers can counsel effectively. Counselling requires a range of specialist behavioural skills which can be acquired

through training, as well as a range of specialist qualities for more in-depth problems. We need to know our
limitations, and when to refer on. Listening to someone
complain about their spouse's reluctance to decorate
the dining room or their son's poor performance in
school examinations is a little different to helping an
individual address a range of psychosexual problems or
dealing with a traumatised employee who has just
heard he has lost his job.

This chapter will:

- state why counselling is necessary in the workplace
- list the range of probems that may require counselling
- list and address some of a manager's concerns about
  counselling
- list the main benefits of counselling
- list and describe a range of personal qualities, skills
  and techniques required by a counsellor
- describe how to set up, conduct and conclude a counselling interview.

Employees with problems are a concern to employers
when they:

- lack concentration and are more likely to make
  mistakes
- are less tolerant and short-tempered with their work-
  mates
- lack confidence and self-esteem because they feel
  unable to cope
- are less productive because their minds are not
  entirely on work
- are sometimes absent from work or are poor time-
  keepers because of conflicting pressues of home and
  work responsibilities

These pressures can result in poor physical and mental
health.

Such problems are clearly debilitating and lead to a decline in personal productivity.

In short, employees' unresolved problems, whether home- or work-related, cost industry millions of pounds a year in absenteeism, lost productivity and decreased efficiency.

In today's world of rapid change, individuals are having to cope with increasing pressures, and this results in stress of one form or another. Whilst many causes of stress are work-related – simple overwork being one of the commonest – the prime cause of stress outside the workplace is relationship problems. But, as already stated, problems from home spill into the workplace and problems from the workplace spill into home life, so that a strained relationship will be strained even further.

Figure 4.1 demonstrates the cost of stress and also the increasing problems caused by relationship difficulties in marriage.

Fig. 4.1 Some statistics on stress and divorce rates

Stress at work costs US industry 10% of GNP each year.
      The National Institute of Occupational Safety & Health, US

Occupational stress causing sickness alone costs £4 billion each year.

                                              UK Health & Safety Executive

Divorce: Rates per 1,000 married couples, England and Wales

1961	1971	1981	1991	1995
2.1	5.9	11.9	13.5	13.2

Office for National Statistics (adapted)

What is counselling?

The definitions of counselling are numerous, but the following give a firm indication of its scope.

> 'a set of techniques, skills and attitudes to help people manage their own problems using their own resources'
>
> REDDY, 1987

> 'the task of counselling is to give the client an opportunity to explore, discover and clarify ways of living more resourcefully and towards greater well-being'
>
> BRITISH ASSOCIATION OF COUNSELLING, 1988

The word 'counsellor' is derived from the Latin *consilium*, a word whose principal meaning is an assembly where people consulted, exchanged views and opinions, discussed and planned. This suggests that people have always used others as a sounding-board to find solutions to their own particular problems. 'No man is an island,' said John Donne.

For most of the time, people adopt strategies for coping with their own particular set of problems, but at some stage in life they have to look beyond their usual resources to deal with overload. This is hardly surprising in a fast-moving, constantly changing world where the individual may be confronted with any number of the following major problems, and others besides:

● Employment: redundancy, dismissal, relocation, long-term sick leave, relationships with colleagues, anxiety over performance, commuting difficulties

- Family: aged/ailing parents, divorce, separation, children, violence in the home, financial hardship, illness, in-laws, sex
- Relationships: partners/neighbours, racial/sexual harrassment
- Housing: repossession, homelessness, burglary, flood, fire
- Finance: over-commitment, debt, bankruptcy
- Substance abuse: alcohol, drugs
- Health: Physical/mental illness
- Emotional problems: depression, anxiety, trauma, bereavement, loss
- Crime: prosecution, arrest, victim of crime, car theft

The manager, as a workplace counsellor, cannot *and should not* try to replace the professional counsellor, but the manager as a workplace counsellor can:

- offer useful support to others in a one-to-one situation
- help others become more effective
- learn to recognise signs of stress in others
- take time to listen
- be approachable
- be attentive
- ensure confidentiality

By offering these skills of first-line counselling, the manager can make a non-intrusive intervention which can often avoid a crisis and will usually improve performance in the workplace.

Managers' concerns about counselling at work

Some managers are understandably cautious about taking on the counselling role because they see it as being in conflict with their management role of monitoring performance and achieving targets. As parents we console, support, nurture, reprimand and discipline as appropriate to the child's needs and the situation. We consider this approach to be good parenting. In the same way, management skills and behaviours need to be appropriate to the situation in order to be effective. Developing counselling skills helps the manager to further develop the skills of effective communication which translate to any situation involving people.

Workplaces tend to be task-orientated rather than people-orientated. This is perhaps another reason that managers may be disinclined to take on the counselling role, because they believe it will increase their own workload. This is not true. Time invested now pays dividends later. Counselling helps people to find their own solution to their own problem and helps them along the path to greater empowerment. The problem always belongs to the counselled, not the counsellor.

Another barrier to counselling at work is that managers fear that they might find themselves out of their depth. That may be so, in which case the best course would be to refer the problem on to experts who can help. Whatever the circumstances, at least the manager will be made aware of the problem and be able to initiate a solution.

Benefits of counselling in the workplace

These can be summarised as follows:

- reduces unhappiness and discontent
- increases efficiency and productivity
- improves working relationships
- increases confidence and self-esteem
- facilitates growth, personal and professional development
- increases confidence and trust in management

- prevents a problem becoming a crisis. In fact, it can create an *opportunity* for the owner of the problem.

Personal qualities needed to counsel in the workplace

The counsellor needs to be:

- open and approachable – able to make someone feel at ease and not threatened
- empathetic – willing to relate to the feelings others are experiencing
- concerned – having a genuine interest and willingness to help and support
- attentive – giving full, individual attention to another person so that they feel they have been heard
- composed – making a thoughtful and considered response; giving importance to the issue without under- or over-reaction
- trustworthy – having integrity and responding to others honestly and respecting confidentiality
- observant – recognising whether others are 'drowning, not waving' by being sensitive to changes in appearance or behaviour which might indicate a problem
- wise – having the understanding or the experience to offer useful support and knowing their own limitations (knowing when to refer on/seek help from outside the workplace).

Setting up an interview

A counselling session can be initiated either by the manager or the person with the problem. Spotting problems is not easy, as people often conceal them because they feel it might suggest they cannot cope and that this will attract management disapproval. The manager, therefore, needs to create an environment that encourages people to share problems in the knowledge that they will be offered help, not disapproval. Managers also have to develop a sensitivity and awareness of the people in their workforce so that they pick up a change in behaviour or appearance that may signal a problem.

In an open, supportive environment where people are aware that help will be offered, then the manager may be approached by a colleague of the one who needs help. In this situation, the manager should create a counselling opportunity by making an approach to the individual concerned. If the individual is resistant to your concern and your attempts to help them, then back off for the present but offer to be available, if required, in the future.

The individual who approaches the manager with, 'I wonder if you could spare me a few minutes,' has created the ideal opening. If this doesn't happen, an appropriate opening would be when the person is alone and the manager can offer help in privacy: 'I've noticed that you seem rather tired lately, John. Is there anything I can help you with? Perhaps we could have a chat?'

Once the opportunity has been created then it is important to find somewhere where you can have the discussion in private and free from interruptions.

Conducting a counselling session

Counselling must be private, confidential and unhurried in order to be effective. The person being counselled needs to feel free to talk and the manager can only listen and be attentive if free from distractions. As a rule of thumb, a counselling session needs to be about 30–45 minutes. The session, or series of sessions, needs to have a shape to it and a recommended framework is Carkhuff's Three-Stage model:

- Exploration of the problem, which can only be achieved by getting the interviewee to talk.
- Understanding – here the counsellor helps the interviewee to think through their problem and put it in perspective.
- Action – this involves helping the individual identify their own solution and take responsibility for implementation.

The Three-Stage model outlines *what* you should do. The next section will concentrate on *how* you should achieve this by describing a range of appropriate skills and techniques.

Skills needed

Establishing rapport. There are a number of ways of doing this. First we need to offer reassurance and put the interviewee at ease by being empathetic and ensuring confidentiality. The interviewee also needs to know that you are offering support, and not being judgmental.

Prompting, open questions. The next skills is to get the interviewee to talk by asking open questions.
  'How did you feel about that?'
  'What happened then?'
  'How did you find out about that?'

Listening. Having got the interviewee to talk, perhaps the most important skill is listening. 'I wasn't able to do much except listen,' is the self-critical remark often made by those new to counselling. *Never underestimate the effectiveness of really listening to someone who knows they are being heard*. There are few situations in life when we have the opportunity to be really listened to by someone willling to give us their undivided attention for half an hour. Listening is the most neglected of our communication skills. Research has shown that people with normal hearing retain only an average of 25% of the spoken word. It is the first skill learned and the least taught. Of the interview situations, the counselling interview, above all, requires more listening than talking, so in this chapter we devote more space to the skill of listening than to the other interviewing skills, which are covered in other chapters.

Why we are poor listeners?

Why, then, are we poor listeners? The following factors may give us some indication:

- We perceive listening to be passive and find concentration difficult.
- The average person speaks at a rate of 130 words per minute and thinks at a rate of 500 words per minute. In consequence, our minds jump ahead of what is being said.
- We listen selectively and shut out anything we regard as unimportant.
- Lack of interest in the subject of conversation lends itself to 'mental walkabout'.
- The listener is tense with emotion, which impairs the ability to listen.
- The listener's mind is full of concerns which cause a block.
- Physical noises intrude and detract from the speaker, e.g. music, television, other people's conversations, traffic noises.
- The listener is mentally preparing what he is going to say rather than concentrating on what is being said.
- The listener has some hearing impairment or is unwell.

- The listener uses a different vocabulary to the speaker and has a different understanding and perception.
- The listener has preconceived ideas which he or she is desperate to retain.

How can we improve our listening?

We can do this in the following ways:

(a) By recognising that listening is an active, not a passive, activity.
(b) By physically attending, which involves:
  - facing the speaker squarely
  - good eye contact
  - open posture
  - leaning towards the speaker
  - being relatively relaxed.
(c) By mentally clearing the mind of our own emotional agenda and personal concerns.
(d) By ensuring the environment is conducive to listening and free from distracting noises and interruptions.
(e) By psychologically attending, which means concentrating on three things:
  - what is being said
  - how it is being said
  - what is not being said.
(f) By reflecting
(g) By summarising
(h) By asking questions.

The counsellor listening to a person relate a problem can easily fall into the trap of hearing the storyline rather than hearing the message. A counsellor learns to listen for the central theme rather than simply concentrating on the 'facts'.

A good listener keeps an open mind and does not

judge the message until it is fully understood; nevertheless, the speaker needs confirmation that he or she is being heard. The problems associated with the speaker being unsure of being heard and perceived correctly are illustrated by a notice which is displayed in the Pentagon:

> 'I know you believe you understand what you think I said, but I am not sure you realise that what you heard is not what I meant.'

Children, at an early age, recognise that listening and hearing are not the same thing. They demand confirmation that their message has been listened to, and often take precautions to ensure that you listen to them by making sure of your attention in advance of speaking. A common way they do this is by touching the person they wish to speak to and addressing them by name: 'Mrs Jones, have you seen Sarah?' If Mrs Jones does not respond, the address will be used again ('Mrs Jones?') until she makes it clear she is giving her attention. When Mrs Jones responds by saying, 'Yes, John,' John is reassured that he is heard and continues the conversation.

Children will not allow a lack of response. This is evident when they reach the joke-telling age and invariably finish with, 'Did you get it?' In adult conversation, we seldom admit to not having understood. In the counselling role you need to check your understanding, and ensure you are getting the correct message.

Listening to, and understanding, the message

Look at Figure 4.2. As you listen to the individual's problem, you can communicate understanding in terms of their experiences, behaviours and feelings. The experience will be related verbally, the behaviour and the emotional effect will be also evident in the client's non-verbal communication.

Fig. 4.2 Listening framework

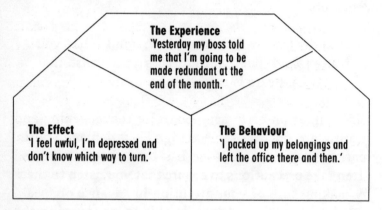

The Experience
'Yesterday my boss told me that I'm going to be made redundant at the end of the month.'

The Effect
'I feel awful, I'm depressed and don't know which way to turn.'

The Behaviour
'I packed up my belongings and left the office there and then.'

Reading and using body language

Being observant to the individual's body language and facial expressions can sometimes provide a clearer indication of feeling than what is being said. As an American commedian once said, 'When someone asks you how you are and you say, 'Fine,' don't forget to tell your face.' Many people do forget!

Be aware of:

- facial expression, smiles, frowns, eyebrow movements
- posture, stance, body movements, hand movements
- voice pitch, tone, inflection level, spacing of words, silences, emphasis
- automatic physical responses, blushing, paleness, pupil dilation, grooming, dress, etc.

Body language or non-verbal communication is generally more spontaneous and less easily controlled than words, which are selected after a conscious thought process. Non-verbal communication can confirm or deny what is being said. For example, 'I feel fine,' spoken with drooping shoulders and quivering lip, is denying his or her own feelings, perhaps transmitting what the individual thinks the counsellor/manager wants to hear. Whereas 'I feel fine,' spoken with a smile and upward tone of voice, is a confirmation of the verbalised message.

Reading body language and non-verbal communication requires close observation and practice. It is not our intention to write a dictionary of gestures and their interpretations, but rather to give an overview of how the body language and gestures of counsellor and counselled enables or inhibits effective communication in the counselling process.

It is our view that body language is not an exact science, and that there is a danger in reading too much into individual gestures, thereby losing the message. We can suffer from 'analysis paralysis'. But managers can become more aware of how we communicate ourselves to others and how we receive their communications. As counsellors, we invite individuals to communicate and relate to us. We issue that invitation verbally but need to reinforce the message non-verbally. So we must:

- Face the client squarely in a position that indicates interest and involvement. If the individual appears uncomfortable or threatened, adopt a position slightly angled away from them.
- Adopt an open posture. Limbs crossed and arms folded across the body indicate lack of involvement and form a barrier in the western culture. Open palms issue an invitation and indicate honesty and acceptance. Be comfortable and aware of how the individual receives non-verbal indicators from you.

- Lean slightly forward. This posture demonstrates interest and willingness to listen. Slouching backward shows a withdrawal of interest, and hands behind head indicates an air of superiority or arrogance that this is all really 'beneath you'. But lunging too far forward can be misinterpreted as aggression and is associated with the issuing of challenges. Be flexible and show facial response to indicate acceptance of what is being said.
- Maintain good eye contact. Steady eye contact is usual for those engaging in serious conversation in the Western culture. Eye contact is a way of saying, 'I'm with you.' Wandering eyes show uninterest and reluctance to become involved. Obvious discomfort in maintaining eye contact can be an indication of a discomfort with closeness in general.

It is important for the counsellor to appear interested, confident, attentive and relaxed. These four guidelines should ensure that. There are no hard and fast rules. All skills take time and practice, but with practice you will do it naturally. Remember how you have internalised your actions in driving a car or using a keyboard? It seems that the skills will never come together and the greater your anxiety the more mistakes you are likely to make. Practise the skills with a colleague or friend in everyday conversation until you feel comfortable and they simply become a natural part of you.

Helpful techniques for the counsellor

Reflecting
When an individual has made a statement, reflect it back to them as a question. e.g. Statement made by interviewee:

'My parents are both elderly and unwell and I feel unable to cope with checking in on them everyday.'
Reflective question from counsellor:
'So you feel that you are under pressure at home and find it more difficult to cope with your work at the moment?'

Reflecting back helps the interviewee examine and acknowledge their feelings. The counsellor then needs to be human by permitting the feelings.
e.g. Counsellor:

'It must be very worrying for you having to cope with so many things at once.'

Towards the end of the exploration it is helpful to summarise.

Summarising
By summarising or paraphrasing what has been said, the counsellor can check their understanding of the situation.

e.g. 'What you seem to be saying is that ...'

Being non-judgmental
Accept what the interviewee has said without expressing personal opinion or criticism. You *can* offer information:

e.g. 'You can get financial help from ...'

Ask questions that move the interviewee towards finding their own solution:

e.g. 'Is there any way you could avoid that in the future?'

'What do you think your options are?'

'How would you like to change that?'

Always remember that the *interviewee owns the problem* and therefore the responsibility for its solution. The counsellor's role is to enable the interviewee to 'untangle' the problem and move on to a solution.

Concluding a counselling session

At the end of the session agree an action plan and set a review date. This helps to clarify things for the interviewee and gives a timeframe.

e.g.   'So you will check with your doctor to see if your parents can get someone to help with their meals, and we will meet next Wednesday at 1.30 pm to see how things are progressing.'

Make it clear that you are available if they need to talk in the future and re-affirm the confidentiality of what has been said.

After a counselling session

- *Do not* make any notes other than to note the date of any subsequent session agreed.
- *Do not* treat the counselled any differently in the presence of other colleagues or make any reference to the interview.
- *Do not* betray confidences – you will never be trusted again.
- *Do* be open and available for further requests for interviews.
- *Do* compile a list of helping agencies and counselling services. Information on these is available from the Citizens' Advice Bureau, your local library and your telephone directory.

Remember, 'A problem shared is a problem halved.' You have made a difference by being there and listening.

Summary

Counselling in the workplace can help people find their own solutions to their own problems. People who successfully manage their own problems are more confident, effective and efficient, both in and out of the workplace.

Managers can become effective workplace counsellors by:

- being approachable
- taking the opportunity to set up a counselling interview
- being aware of the skills needed, especially the importance of listening
- learning the techniques of conducting a counselling interview
- being aware of outside helping agencies
- respecting confidentiality.

5

The Giving Bad News Interview

This interview, which is part of a manager's lot from time to time, is another one that is not relished. In fact, often when bad news has to be given, many managers avoid it and in the process do more harm to the recipient than if they had bitten the bullet and delivered the bad news.

In the workplace the giving of bad news will probably relate to one of the following:

- redundancy
- a denied promotion
- the denial of a requested transfer
- an unsuccessful examination result
- the turning down of a holiday request on requested dates.

When faced with a bad news situation, managers may respond in one of the following ways:

- They avoid the issue, pretending it hasn't happened, or it will go away.
- They hope the recipient will hear it from someone else, or from another source. How often have people who have been made redundant heard the news on the radio or from a letter left discreetly on their desk?
- They impart the news over the telephone, followed by information that they are away for the next three weeks in Bali.

- They get someone else to do it because they can't face it.
- They confront the individual and 'give it to them straight', in a direct, if not blunt, manner.
- They confront the individual and deliver the news in a calm, unemotive and sensitive way, dealing with reactions in an appropriate manner.

How many managers can put their hand on their heart and say they fit into the last category?

The giving of bad news in the workplace, for any of the reasons stated above, needs also to be seen in context. Is the conveying of news relating to the above as bad or formidable as the situations that our colleagues in the police force and medical professions face as part of their duties? Is telling someone their holiday request has been turned down as bad as telling a patient that they are terminally ill and have only a short time to live? Or informing parents at two o'clock in the morning that their son has been knocked down by a car and advising them to prepare themselves for the worst?

Later in the chapter, two case studies relating to the medical profession will be given. These are true stories and demonstrate clearly that certain principles need to be observed when giving bad news, whatever the situation. Hopefully, the reader will have to conduct bad news interviews in less unpleasant situations.

Objectives

The giving bad news interview is never going to be easy. At the end, the 'feel good factor' is not a realistic objective. What, then, is realistic? The objectives will vary according to the situation but they will probably include all or some of the following:

- To get the recipient to accept the news without any long-term bitterness and cynicism, which they could turn inward on themselves, or outward towards the manager and the organisation. If the individual is remaining in the organisation, they could turn their attention to spreading discord, reducing morale and taking every opportunity to 'throw a spanner in the works'. If the individual is leaving the organisation, they could carry such a huge chip on their shoulder that they will wage a long crusade amongst their network of contacts, both social and professional, to rubbish the organisation.
- If we cannot get total acceptance of the news, or do anything to change things, then the interview itself has to be a *damage-limitation* exercise.
- To keep our own self-respect and the respect of the recipient and colleagues. The recipient is not going to like the news, but may respect us for conveying the news in a caring and empathetic manner.
- To look to the future and to explore ways of making an opportunity out of a disappointment or setback. Access to future support services can be outlined. This would apply in the case of redundancy.
- To make as good a job of it as we can, possibly improve on last time, and not get flustered if things don't go smoothly.

Ultimately, managers can only hope to handle the situation to the best of their abilities and hope that positives will emerge from a difficult situation. The following quotation, relating to the medical profession, aptly summarises this hope:

'The task of bearing bad news is a testing ground for the entire range of our professional skills and

abilities – if we do it badly the patients or fami-
lies may never forgive us; if we do it well, they
will never forget us.'

ROBERT BUCKMAN

Why bad news is bad news

Giving the bad news itself is not the problem. It is not
actually difficult to say any of the following: 'Your
transfer to another department has been turned down.'
Or, 'Your promotion application was carefully considered by the panel, but on this occasion they have
decided to turn it down.' Or, 'Your request for holiday
leave in the first two weeks in July has been denied.' Or,
'The Company has gone through a considerable downsizing operation in recent months in response to
adverse market conditions and your post has been a
casualty of the reorganisation.'

The real problem relates to *ourselves*, for the following reasons:

- We recognise our own shortcomings in the situation
  we find ourselves in. We know it is difficult, we may
  not have done it before and, if we have, we may have
  done it badly or have unpleasant recollections.
- We know that the news will cause discomfort, disappointment, etc., to the recipient and we don't like
  seeing this at close quarters.
- We dislike remaining at close quarters in the same
  room as someone who is dealing with unpleasantness.
- We fear we will be blamed for the situation which,
  in most cases, is beyond our control. It is human
  nature to seek a scapegoat or 'someone to kick' as the
  object of our frustrations, so who better than the
  person who delivers the bad news? Who wants to be
  a parking attendant who usually gets a mouthful for

our inability to comply with well-publicised regulations?

- We fear the unpredictability of the reactions of the recipient and our ability to cope and deal with them. This is probably the main concern: the recipient's reaction could be acute. Possible reactions are numerous and include the following:

dismay	denial
despair	guilt
anxiety	humour
shock	fear
anger and aggression	disbelief

The interview structure

The interview has two major components:

- giving the information
- dealing with, and responding to, the recipient's reactions.

The two are inseparable.

Before the interview

Like all the other interviews, thorough preparation is essential. Again, preparation is no guarantee of success (whatever that might be in this case) but it increases the chances that the interview will not be an unmitigated disaster giving no possibility of exploring positive future developments.

The following therefore need to be addressed:

- Make the usual arrangements relating to privacy and allow for plenty of time. This interview could transform itself into a lengthy Counselling Interview.
- Consider the individual and *their likely responses* to the

news and how *you* are going to react to them. You can also consider whether you need readily available support either in the form of counselling services or for your own physical protection. A diminutive person would be ill-advised to conduct a bad news interview in an isolated room or building with a seventeen-stone heavyweight with a history of assault.

- Make sure you have all the information relating to the situation and the reasons for the decision made. Almost the first verbal response is likely to be, 'Why?' In just the same way, patients in receipt of really tragic news relating to accidents or medical conditions ask, 'Why me?'
- If there are future options available to the recipient, be sure you know the support that might be available.
- Write down precisely *what* you are going to say and *how* you are going to say it at the start. This will give you confidence and, as in all situations, confidence breeds competence.
- Identify the recipient's agenda and yours but give priority to *their* agenda. Below is a good example, taken from the medical profession, of the dangers of getting your priorities wrong.

> The following story was told by the widow of the patient, Ted Johnson. 'Ted had come from the hospital and they had told him that he had a bad heart and that it was very serious. Our family doctor was young and he came round to see us before breakfast about a week later. He kept on repeating that Ted had to draw up his will and should get on with it quickly. We kept on saying we'd done all that, but he kept on saying we'd have to hurry, things were getting worse very quickly. I found out later from another patient in the hospital that the doctor had had two conver-

sations with Ted like that already while he was in hospital. After that breakfast session Ted just went silent and hardly spoke to me till he died. He went from being a bouncy, cheerful businessman to being a silent, brooding wreck. He died nearly a year ago and every time I think of him I remember that breakfast interview with the doctor and it makes me cry.'

How to Break Bad News: A Guide for Health Care
Professionals by Robert Buckman © 1992.
Macmillan General Books, UK;
University of Toronto Press, Canada;
Johns Hopkins Press, Baltimore, USA.
Reproduced with permission of the
author and publishers.

Whilst it is recognised that such dire and extreme examples don't occur in the workplace, this story does emphasise the point. The pathological grief exhibited by the surviving wife had overridden some happy memories that must exist. Not much damage-limitation here!

During the interview

You have written your carefully worded opening, so use it. It should be brief, clear, unambiguous, and you should appear sympathetic. Don't precede this with a lot of social chit-chat – you owe it to the recipient to get to the point fairly quickly. The bad news itself could cause disappointment or distress, but a supportive and sympathetic interviewer *may* minimise the amount of pain felt eventually. The recipient, whilst disliking the news, may not equally dislike you if you appear calm, composed and professional. You may even earn their respect.

During the interview you must be acutely aware of your body language and the messages it transmits. Most importantly, you must establish eye contact. Your voice should be calm, clear and not raised. Don't fidget or twiddle as this communicates nervousness and can irritate your interviewee.

You might initiate a bad news interview as follows:

'John, I'd like you to come and see me for a few minutes. There is something we need to talk about regarding the holiday request you've made.'

And continue:

'I see you've made an application for holiday leave for the period 14–28 July. I'm really sorry that I'll have to disappoint you on this one. Unfortunately, so many other people applied for these dates before you did that if I agreed to your request it would leave the department very short-staffed. We wouldn't be able to function properly.

'However, and this is the only thing I can suggest to you, if you managed to negotiate a swap with someone else in the department, then please get back to me. I'm afraid I can't agree to your request as things stand at the moment. Perhaps in future it's worth bearing in mind that applications for leave should be made well in advance if you want a busy and popular holiday period.'

The giving of the bad news is the easiest part of the interview. The real skill lies in coping with the interviewee's reactions. For a start, what follows could be unpredictable and therefore we are unsure how we'll have to react. Secondly, the range of reactions outlined earlier require a number of different behavioural responses. However, if we have done our homework on the individual concerned we should have eliminated a large element of the unpredictability.

For difficult responses the interviewer *must* stay as

calm, assertive and composed as possible. There are three main guidelines:

- give as much leeway as you can
- stay calm and composed and don't raise your voice
- be understanding and empathetic but be assertive.

The more difficult the situation, the more important it is to stick to these three basic rules. The interviewer must try to take one step back from the situation until the time has arrived to move forward.

There are generally four kinds of response from the recipient of bad news:

- stunned silence
- emotional outburst, notably tears
- aggressive behaviour
- argumentative behaviour.

Stunned silence

This is a common reaction and silence does not give any indication of what the recipient is feeling. The discomfort the silence causes is *your* embarrassment and the damaging effect of pursuing your own agenda has already been illustrated. Whatever your level of discomfort, be patient and wait calmly. The interviewee probably needs time to think and, in due course, you will sense when they are ready to talk. When this time has arrived, encourage them to talk as talking about a problem is in itself therapeutic. Ask open, not closed, questions, don't interrupt and listen empathetically.

Emotional outburst

This, again, is a common reaction and causes discomfort to the interviewer. Tears are probably the main reaction and most of us, irrespective of gender, are not very good at coping with tears from others. A display of tears can be:

- genuine distress, in which case remember that 'a good cry' is therapeutic and marks the first stage in the recovery process
- the first ritual in a game aimed to attract attention and make others feel guilty.

Whatever the reason for the tears, the best tactic is to sit it out and await composure. If tissues are to hand, offer them. If the tears are not genuine, don't succumb to the emotional blackmail (if you know your staff, you should have a clue as to the reason for the tears). Once the distress (or apparent distress) has subsided, encourage the interviewee to talk, in much the same way as you would proceed after stunned silence. The questioning starts to get the interviewee to think about the way forward.

Aggressive behaviour

The most common manifestation of this is the individual who 'rants and raves'. When dealing with this form of behaviour it is important to stay calm and not counter aggression with aggression. It is best to let the storm blow over and assertively point out that the current behaviour is unacceptable for a reasonable discussion. The following is another good example from the medical profession.

> The most aggressive behaviour that I have had to face (other than from patients in the emergency department who were on drugs, or going through a psychotic episode) came from a husband of a woman dying of metastatic melanoma. At the first meeting he swore continuously for several minutes about the hospital,

other doctors, and me, and then began throwing a chair around the room, getting it closer and closer to me. The more he ranted, the more I tried to look calm (I stayed seated, undid my jacket and made sure my shoulders did not hunch up, although I was quite scared) and I told him (when I could) that I would listen to whatever he had to say, but we had to talk as civilised people. When he failed to get a reaction from his violent behaviour he simply stopped and a few minutes later his behaviour – although still florid – was well within the limits of acceptability.'

How to Break Bad News: A Guide for Health Care
Professionals

If, in a situation like the one outlined above, the interviewee doesn't calm down and appears threatening, then call for outside assistance. In a civilised society such recourse should be extremely rare, but if the danger signals are there, don't hesitate to act.

Argumentative behaviour

As with the previous example, don't engage on their terms and, as in all the other cases, stay calm and composed. Keeping your composure helps you to think clearly and it is clarity of thought you need in order to deal with the argumentative individual who will seek to enter a negotiation or offer another, and what he sees as a better, option. This is where your thorough preparation in gathering relevant information pays off. So stand your ground, stick to relevant information, deal calmly with the 'why' question, don't be swayed and don't be led in a direction you don't want to go. In short, *try to act, not react* – act on the basis of relevant information and don't react to the provocation.

When the emotions have been dealt with, there will

come a point when you need to consider moving forward and helping the individual focus on the future. You will usually sense when the time to move has arrived. A good guideline is that people tend to have 'got it all off their chest' when you hear early responses repeated. Having helped the recipient deal with the shock of the news, and start to come to terms with it, we then begin to explore ways of helping them plan for the future and look at the courses of action open to them. The individual may feel that they would like to postpone talking about the future to a later date, which is their prerogative. Alternatively, they may want to start this now. Whatever the timing, a number of things need to be borne in mind:

- The interviewee is often at a low ebb. Their ego may be bruised and their self-esteem may have taken a battering. They may have a great sense of failure. Consequently, be empathetic and help them realise that it is not the end of the world. Far worse things can happen and it may only be a temporary setback.
- Start immediately on helping to build self-esteem and remind the interviewee of all their good qualities.
- Let them know what support is available and explore ways of helping them move forward so that they may be able to create an opportunity out of a crisis.
- Try to offer reassurance, where appropriate, that the emotional outburst you have just been on the receiving end of won't be held against them.

Wherever possible, it is important to try to end on a positive note so that when the interviewee leaves the room they don't see the future as 'all doom and gloom', but see instead that there is hope and something to build on.

After the interview

You will probably need a double brandy or some fresh air, after which try to get back to business as usual. Whilst you should certainly review the experience and learn from it, don't dwell on the situation unduly. You can't become the dumping ground for everyone else's problems and emotions. You can, of course, offer whatever support is appropriate to help them through their problem by helping them to develop their coping skills, which aim to ensure that the learning potential in a crisis or setback is maximised and the distress inevitably caused by the crisis is minimised. A crisis *can* be a significant opportunity for considerable personal development all round.

Summary

The giving bad news interview is one that few, if any, managers relish. It is never going to be easy and often it is a damage-limitation exercise. Ideally, we should aim for the recipient to accept the news whilst at the same time keeping our self-respect and the respect of others.

The giving of the bad news itself is not the main reason we dislike such interviews. Rather, we question our capacity to deal with and respond to the recipient's reactions, which can be unpredictable. It is essential that we prepare thoroughly, not only gathering all relevant information, but anticipating the likely reaction and knowing how to respond accordingly. In dealing with a range of emotional reactions, the interviewer must at all times remain calm and composed and may sometimes have to take a step back from the situation until the storm has passed. The interviewer requires excellent communication skills, especially listening, reflecting and asking open questions. The interviewer's body language must mirror the calm, composed exterior.

When all emotions have been expressed by the interviewee, the interviewer should make a start on helping them focus on the future. They need to keep the news in perspective and understand that, whilst the news may be a setback, it is not the end of the world. Remind them of their positive qualities and explore ways of capitalising on these. A crisis can be a springboard for a big leap forward in the future.

The Feedback Interview

A manager may have to give feedback to an individual in a number of situations. Sometimes, like the Grievance and Disciplinary Interviews, the encounter may be viewed with some trepidation. There is no need to be apprehensive about it, as the necessary steps can be taken to ensure that the risks of the interview going wrong are minimised and that desired outcomes are achieved.

In other chapters the importance of preparation, room arrangement, allowing sufficient time, and so on, have been mentioned. These are important for the Feedback Interview too. Readers should therefore refer to chapter 1.

This chapter will outline some of the main behaviours that you should adopt for interviews set up to give feedback of various kinds. We have chosen three types of situation:

(a) Giving feedback, including feedback from psychometric tests
(b) Giving criticism
(c) Giving praise

General guidelines for giving feedback

The most important point is that the interviewer *should*

focus on the behaviour and not the person. This avoids personal attack and the feedback is reinforcing good behaviours or attempting to change undesired behaviours. Students of learning theory will recognise the importance of positive or negative reinforcement in the conditioning process.

The other main points are as follows:

- Be assertive and aware of your rights as well as the other person's.
- Don't be aggressive or overbearing and don't be non-assertive, apologetic or meek and mild.
- Be direct (not blunt) and to the point and don't 'beat about the bush'.
- Avoid sarcasm and demeaning comments.
- Avoid blaming the individual with aggressive 'you' statements.
- Display appropriate body language, especially in terms of eye contact, body positioning and physical mannerisms.
- Be specific about the good or bad behaviours and non-judgmental.
- Mutually explore and possibly offer suggestions or options for improvement or change.

Feedback from psychometric instruments or skills inventories

Such instruments are now used widely in a number of development situations. Reliability and validity vary, but they are very useful tools to develop individuals and bring about change, both on an individual basis and in a team situation. In many situations, e.g. mental ability tests and personality tests, the scoring relates to a norm which should be specified. With the more in-depth psychometric instruments, test users are trained and certified with the appropriate body, which minimises any potential damage that could be done if feedback is badly handled. Like counselling, it is important to recognise one's own limitations as an interviewer and know when to refer to someone else. The well-intentioned, but poorly trained and poorly skilled Samaritan is not welcome or appreciated.

Feedback from these inventories should not be viewed as an opporunity to 'beat someone over the head', 'put them in their place' or make them realise 'they are not as good as they think they are'. Thus it should be seen not as a judgment or criticism, but as developmental.

Objectives

The objectives of the interview should be:

- ownership of the feedback by the recipient
- a commitment to change where desired
- some contracting of an action plan for implementation after the interview.

The feedback should be a participative exercise where everything that is said will be viewed as helpful and developmental. This means that the feedback should be carried out in a relaxed atmosphere, unhurried, free from tension and characterised by openness and honesty. Statements that are judgmental, accusing and patronising will immediately encounter resistance and a range of defensive behaviours with the result that the objectives of the interview are unlikely to be achieved. Side by side, alongside a table, or across the corner of a table, is often a good seating arrangement when some visual portrayal of test results is needed.

As in the majority of other interviews, it is important to devote time to establishing rapport. The time allowed should vary but it shouldn't be rushed. Whilst individuals are usually fascinated to learn about themselves, self-awareness can be a very threatening process and many recipients are conditioned to view it as a negative and not a positive process: 'It will tell me what I am poor at, not what I am good at.' Experience will tend to suggest when the time to move on has arrived, after which we suggest the following sequence:

1 Explain the test and how the feedback will be given. Some of the points made when the test was taken may be repeated here. A written report could follow at the end of the interview and, if this is intended, say so.

2 Give the feedback by:
   • being open, honest and non-judgmental
   • not taking a patronising or 'critical parent' role
   • checking for understanding by asking open and probing questions
   • allowing time for resistance, as part of the feedback may come as a surprise and may require time for assimilation
   • not becoming defensive yourself.
   A number of useful phrases are:
      'The profile indicates that ...'
      'The indications are that ...'
      'Measured against this occupational group norm the score suggests ...'
   Unhelpful phrases are:
      'You are ...'
      'This is a poor score on ...'
      'One area of weakness is ...'
      'I've very rarely seen a score this low.'

3 Work with the positives. There should be quite a number!

4 Explore weaknesses or development areas by:

a) letting the recipient identify the poor score or weakness
b) exploring solutions and/or actions
c) considering the benefits of change
d) mutually exploring options or possible avenues for development
e) obtain (if appropriate) a commitment to change with the recognition that if change is possible, the onus is on the interviewee
f) enquire as to the level of support required from the organisation which could involve yourself as interviewer or manager

Remember: It's not what you say, but how you say it!

Giving criticism

Many managers view giving criticism in the same light as giving bad news. They are apprehensive about the response as well as their own feelings. Many are also conditioned to view criticism in a negative light, seeing only the destructive effects and not the constructive benefits. Unlike feedback, criticism can be judgmental, but like the feedback interview, the main objectives are to gain acceptance and to bring about a change in behaviour. Therefore we re-emphasise the point that the interviewer should focus on behaviour and not the person. Many positive benefits can accrue from properly administered constructive criticism.

It is important to undertake all the usual preparatory tasks relating to timing, privacy and information-gathering. Give some thought also to likely questions and objections and prepare your likely responses. Tell yourself that you must stay calm and collected and not react in an emotional way to any provocation.

It may be helpful for you either to mentally rehearse

your approach, particularly the opening, even to write out your opening and possibly repeat it to yourself several times so that it is very familiar to you and you say it naturally. You should aim to give the criticism as early as possible in the interview, hence the importance of preparing the wording or your opening comments extremely carefully.

At the interview it is advisable to:

- Get to the point quickly
- Be specific. You should state what the problem is and, where appropriate, how the problem is affecting you. Example: 'A number of estimates you've done for me recently have been incorrect so that in the ensuing managers' meeting I was made to look a fool when colleagues checked the calculations.' Or, 'You've been late on several occasions in the past month and this is causing me a problem in insisting on good time-keeping with the rest of the staff.' As in the Disciplinary Interview, you should have specific facts at your disposal to support your comments.
- Own what you say. Use the 'I' word and take responsibility for what you are saying. These sorts of phrases are usually appropriate:
  'I want ...'
  'I think ...'
  'I would like ...'
  'I don't like ...'
  'I know that ...'
- Use assertive body language. A loud voice, finger-wagging, inability to look the recipient in the eye, signifying either aggressive or non-assertive behaviour, are *not* recommended. People are much more comfortable if you look at them directly and in a calm, unemotional manner. Remember 'weak views, forcibly expressed' won't achieve much.

- Explore suggestions for improvement. Whilst you should know what you want in terms of outcome, you can ask for suggestions from the recipient first before suggesting your own. They may well suggest what you want, which will increase ownership. Phrases like:

  'What do you think we should do?'

  'How can we resolve this?'

  'Let's consider the options.'

  are usually appropriate and will, hopefully, lead on to agreement to get the desired change.

After the interview, only a few tasks need to be completed. Nothing needs to be written up, but you need to make a mental note of the problem and check periodically that the desired change has happened. You want to avoid having to go down the disciplinary route.

You should also review the experience as a valuable learning vehicle. If you handled the interview to your satisfaction, congratulate yourself and analyse why. Equally, if there is room for improvement, review your mistakes and learn from them. Openness and honesty with yourself are just as important as openness and honesty with your interviewee!

Giving praise

Whilst giving praise is a more palatable task than giving criticism, it can still cause embarrassment to both the giver and the recipient. We are perhaps concerned with our own feelings and also the possible embarrassed reaction of the recipient. We want the recipient to accept the praise as sincere and to use it to reinforce good work or behaviour so that it continues and motivation levels increase.

Most of the points relating to giving praise are similar

to those for giving criticism but with a different emphasis. The main points to remember are:

- Do all the usual preparations in terms of timing, room
  preparation, privacy and information-gathering. In
  the same way that 'bawling someone out in public'
  for undesired behaviour can cause embarrassment, so
  can a gushing round of praise in public.
- Write down your opening statement and rehearse it
  until you know it well. Practise with someone else
  (spouse at home?) if it helps.
- Deliver the praise as soon as possible.
- Be specific by saying exactly what pleased you and
  how it affected you. Example: 'All the estimates
  you've done for me this past month have been accurate, well presented and accepted by the management
  team, which has reflected well on the department and
  myself.'
- Be sincere. Keep it short and to the point. Don't gush
  and go over the top, as this may be perceived as insin-
  cere, and don't adopt a patronising manner as that
  will irritate the recipient.
- Own what you say. Use the 'I' word and take responsibility for what you are saying. So, 'The company
  would like to place on record its appreciation of ...' is
  not as good as:
      'I would like to ...'
      'I appreciate ...'
- Use assertive body language.

As for afterwards, all that needs to be done is to
review the encounter and learn from it.

Summary

Some of the main points of this chapter are:

- Giving feedback to individuals, for whatever reason, can be a potential source of embarrassment for managers.
- All feedback should focus on the behaviour and not the person.
- The objective of all feedback is to gain acceptance from the recipient and for it to be developmental.
- Feedback should be direct and specific.
- With giving criticism and praise, own the feedback: use 'I', which is owning, not 'you', which is blaming.
- Use every interview as a learning experience for yourself by reviewing your success and failures.

7

The Grievance Interview

The Grievance Interview can be defined as one in which a manager meets an employee who is dissatisfied with something about the organisation. It could therefore be a situation in which the employee is dissatisfied with a decision or work practice of their immediate line manager, with the line manager having to conduct the interview. If the interview between employee and line manager fails to resolve the issue then the grievance can be taken up the line, with the employee having the right to go to the highest level if the need is felt.

Many managers may well view Grievance Interviews in the same distasteful light as Disciplinary Interviews because they can generate emotional behaviours and open conflict. Commonsense, rational thinking and objectivity can go out of the window when personal agendas and emotive reactions surface. But there the similarity ends.

The major difference between the Disciplinary and the Grievance Interview is that whereas the former is manager-initiated, the latter is employee-initiated. The employee may arrive at the interview in a highly agitated and emotional state, in which case there is some similarity with the Counselling Interview in that the manager must draw on skills of defusing emotion, listening, summarising, possibly empathy, and mutual exploration. See chapter 4, page 86.

When an individual comes forward with a grievance the manager has two options:

1   See the individual immediately.
2   Insist on a delay before conducting the interview.

A third course of action, refusing to see the person, is not an option because employees have the right by law to air their grievances. A grievance procedure should exist in the organisation so if one is not in existence it needs to be instituted, and quickly. Option 1 may be the best option if the heat needs to be taken out of the situation quickly. Option 2 is probably the more sensible course, provided the delay is short. A long delay can exacerbate the problem in that a discontent, like a wound, can fester and get worse without attention. A short delay can allow the manager time for composure and also to make a few discreet inquiries in order to get the full picture. Forewarned is forearmed.

As a general rule, therefore, the grievance should be dealt with quickly and at the lowest level possible. The longer it lasts and the higher up the organisation it goes, the more the parties tend to polarise and the more difficult it becomes to achieve a resolution. Furthermore, the more time (and money) is lost, the more people become vulnerable to a loss of face upon resolution. In short, the grievance should be 'nipped in the bud'.

Objectives

These are as follows:

1   To enable the employee to air the complaint.
2   To listen to and understand the nature of the grievance.
3   To explore the reasons for dissatisfaction and, where possible, remove them.

4   To obtain a speedy resolution to the problem.
5   To ensure against a repetition of the circumstances which led up to the grievance.
6   In the event of an unsuccessful resolution, to inform the person with the grievance of their rights to take it further and the procedure for doing so.

Managers, like subordinates with a grievance, do sometimes become stubborn and intransigent about the situation, letting personal agendas and emotions get in the way of commonsense and the need for an outcome. Consequently they approach the grievance interview with a closed mind and objective number 6 and not objective number 4 as the goal. In conflict management terms, they should seek a win/win situation and not a win/lose.

Before the interview

As in the Counselling Interview, there is often little preparation that can be done.

The worst scenario is that a highly emotive individual with a grievance appears at the door without warning, demanding an immediate interview. However, managers can act against this eventuality by:

1   Keeping their ear to the ground and being aware of events in their work area so that surprises don't emerge 'out of the blue'.
2   Once they have been alerted via the grapevine, discreetly obtaining relevant background information.
3   Steering the interview into a quiet place, free from interruptions: like other interviews, the grievance interview shouldn't be conducted in public.
4   Being familiar with the organisation's grievance

procedure and the limits of their own authority in handling the grievance. If the grievance has to go further, being aware of the procedure beyond them and what the individual's rights are, particularly with regard to representation.

5   Developing on-the-job counselling skills to deal with individuals with a problem. Counselling skills are very effective in defusing a potentially volatile and emotional situation.

During the interview

Unlike most other interviews, here it is not advisable to spend time trying to establish rapport with a few rounds of polite social chit-chat. The individual with the grievance will want to get it off their chest. However trivial or trite the grievance may seem to you it is important to them, so don't be dismissive, pour scorn on the issue or try to evade it.

At the outset, the interviewee may be in a highly emotional state. The interviewer must try and remain calm and composed and give the interviewee the time required to get things off their chest. When the interviewee has calmed down, the interviewer can begin the *investigative* stage of the interview. A simple, open question along the lines of, 'What appears to be the problem?' should usually get the proceedings under way nicely, unless, of course, the problem has been outlined in the initial dialogue. As in the Counselling Interview, the 'presenting problem' may not be the 'real problem', so the interviewer must listen very carefully. By skilful dovetailing of probing questions, summarising and reflecting, the interviewer should be able to get to the heart of the matter. Be prepared for the fact that the Grievance Interview could turn itself into a Counselling Interview.

The objective of the interview, after the initial stage, is to resolve the problem. There will be instances when a resolution will not be necessary. The interviewee may just have been seeking some attention, or just 'wanting to let rip'. On the other hand, there may be a genuine grievance for which no solution is reached during the interview. In this case the interviewee is informed, if they want to take it further, of the next stage of the grievance procedure. If so, you should send a written statement of the grievance to your own line manager. Your manager is therefore forewarned for the next round.

If a resolution is to be reached, a more client-centred counselling approach may be appropriate so that a number of options are generated and the way forward is agreed. However, if you are part of the interviewee's problem, this approach will almost certainly be inappropriate. Where future action is agreed the interviewer should summarise it.

In concluding the interview, you should thank the interviewee for bringing the matter to your attention, despite any distate you may feel for the situation and relief that the interview is over. Remember that in bringing the grievance out into the open, the interviewee has made you fully aware of the problem, a potential conflict situation has hopefully been resolved so that future working relationships will be improved and the output and effectiveness of the work area should increase.

After the interview

Depending on outcome (1, 2 or 3 below), the following need to be done:

1   When the employee has just 'let off steam' and no

further post-interview follow-up is expected: maintain contact periodically with the employee to see how they are getting on, in the hope of avoiding a recurrence.

2   When the employee and manager reach a mutually agreed resolution: confirm in writing, if appropriate, and agree a follow-up interview at a future date to check on progress.

3   When no resolution is reached and the employee still feels aggrieved: point out the next stage of the grievance procedure, write up notes from the interview as a record and inform your immediate superior so he or she is forewarned.

Summary

Some of the main points in this chapter are:

• Managers usually view Grievance Interviews in the same distasteful light as Disciplinary Interviews.

• The Grievance Interview is unlike most other interviews in that it is subordinate-initiated so that the manager has little time to prepare and could be caught unawares.

• It is most similar to the Counselling Interview in that skills of defusing emotion, empathy, active listening and mutual exploration of solutions are required.

• A grievance should be dealt with quickly and at the lowest level possible.

• Its main objective should be a speedy resolution to the problem, although this is not always possible.

• Every organisation should have a grievance procedure and every manager should be aware of it.

8

The Disciplinary Interview

The *Concise Oxford Dictionary* offers numerous definitions of the word 'discipline' (noun and verb) of which the following are just a few:

trained condition;
order maintained among schoolboys, soldiers, prisoners, etc.;
system of rules for conduct;
control exercised by members of church;
chastisement;
mortification by penance;
bring under control, train to obedience and order.

No doubt many of us can identify with this and, like the authors, were conditioned to see the above as a fair definition. Many of us (particularly the older generation of readers) can identify with school and parental practices in which 'spare the rod and spoil the child' was the ruling maxim and punishment, often corporal, was seen as a deterrent to future, undesired behaviours. Furthermore, many of us have had this idea reinforced either by experiences in more controlled institutions like the ones mentioned or inferred in the above definitions and by the film and television industries, which often depict institutional life in prisons, armed forces, schools, and so on, as one of a harsh, disciplinary regime in which transgression of the desired code of behaviour brings severe and unpleasant punishment. Words such as 'the cane', 'detention', 'imprisonment', 'suspension', 'the sack', 'solitary confinement', all spring to mind.

As child-rearing and educational practices have become more humane and enlightened, so have managerial and supervisory styles in the workplace. In terms of the Disciplinary Interview, this chapter will largely argue that the above definitions are inappropriate and that:

- Discipline is about correction, not necessarily punishment.
- The organisation itself has a responsibility to its employees to have a fair and well-publicised disciplinary procedure in place.
- If a disciplinary situation results in dismissal, then in most (not all) cases, the organisation and management need to look at what can be improved in order to prevent a repetition.
- It is the handling of the disciplinary process, largely through the operation of the organisation's disciplinary procedure and the handling of the interview itself, which is crucial to success or failure.

The chapter will focus upon guidelines for an effective disciplinary procedure as well as on how best to conduct the interview itself. With regard to the guidelines, these will be entirely related to the UK because disciplinary action can, and often does, cross the boundary into matters of law, which obviously vary between countries. Non-UK readers are therefore strongly urged to familiarise themselves with the relevant employment laws and for line managers a good starting point would be the Human Resources Department.

With regard to the conduct of the interview itself, we believe that the interpersonal skills and processes are

appropriate for most, if not all situations, irrespective
of culture. Our experience of running training
programmes across four continents indicates that there
is much common ground in the conducting of the interview itself. The main variables, therefore, are the
organisation's disciplinary procedure and the national
legal framework.

The Rule Book – key principles

Advice on aspects of employment legislation are way
beyond the scope of this book. Nevertheless, managers
handling disciplinary interviews have to work within
the framework of the organisation's disciplinary procedure and this can greatly impact on the effectiveness of
the interview. It is not much use being able to conduct
an excellent disciplinary interview if there is an inappropriate framework to support it.

In the UK, the Advisory, Conciliation and Arbitration
Service (ACAS) provides guidance on good practice in
disciplinary matters. The ACAS Code of Practice on
Disciplinary Practice and Procedures, and an example of
a Disciplinary Procedure are reproduced at the end of
the book as Appendices II and III. Analysis of the ACAS
guidelines, backed by several interviews with legal and
human resources personnel, suggests that the following
key principles apply to the drafting and production of
the Rule Book:

1   Good, *clear* rules and disciplinary procedures help
    both the employer and the employee. Employees
    know where they stand and what is expected in
    terms of attendance, conduct, performance, etc.,
    and what can happen if the required expectations
    are not met.
2   Requirements should be clearly defined by the

manager and *communicated* to employees, so that everyone knows what is expected. Organisations should consider their communication networks. Dumping the Company Personnel Manual and pinning the rules and procedures to a noticeboard in the works canteen may not serve the intended purpose.

3   Rules and procedures should be *familiar to everyone* in the organisation. In view of the potential damage to livelihood and careers that adverse disciplinary outcomes can cause, the disciplinary rules and procedures should automatically be part of any induction programme for all new employees. They should also be repeated for individuals taking their first managerial position, so that new managers fully understand the extent of their authority and what can happen if they don't follow procedure.

4   Procedures thereafter should *always be followed according to the book*. The prime objective of an organisation's disciplinary procedure, certainly in the short term, should not be punishment, but correction and improvement. This is somewhat different from the message behind the definitions quoted at the start of the chapter. Unfortunately, many managers are still so conditioned by their earlier experiences or the need to assert their authority and 'get one over' on someone, that their emotions rule their heads and their sole objective is to punish someone. If, in the long run, the case results in dismissal, it may result in a claim before an Industrial Tribunal. The Company and manager must be in a position to demonstrate that the reason motivating the dismissal, as well as the procedure used to enact the dismissal, was scrupulously fair and consistent. Otherwise the Tribunal may rule in favour of the person dismissed, in which case both

the manager and the organisation are left with 'egg on their face'. Also it is not a very cost-effective way of promoting a good Company image!

5   Rules should *always be applied consistently*. Otherwise the organisation leaves itself open to criticisms of heavy-handedness, discrimination and victimisation, as well as being vulnerable to an unfair dismissal claim at Industrial Tribunal. Furthermore, other members of the workforce see inconsistency as a threat which can cause problems of demotivation, poor morale and low team spirit. A consistently applied disciplinary system, one which is perceived as fair, will earn the respect and confidence of the workforce.

6   Disciplinary action should be carried out *promptly*. Problems tend to escalate if left to fester, so a problem situation should be 'nipped in the bud'. Unfortunately, many managers will not confront the problem, hoping the situation will resolve itself.

7   Accurate *records* should be kept of all disciplinary instances. This has the following benefits:

- Managers can refer back to previous stages with one individual so that if the matter results in dismissal, then the organisation can display consistency and its observation of procedure. In other words, in the event of Industrial Tribunal, the manager and organisation have covered themselves.

- If similar cases arise with other people, managers can refer to records for guidance and procedure and to ensure fairness and consistency. This is not to imply that all similar offences are exactly alike and require the same disciplinary action, as all cases must be treated in isolation and on merit, but it will help achieve consistency.

- Continual occurrence of similar problems may help managers identify deep-seated resentments or inappropriate rules and regulations which may require some modification to obviate the need for disciplinary action in future. A proactive, rather than a reactive, approach can pay dividends.

Points to remember

Of all the interviews that managers may have to conduct, this is the one they least relish. It should also not be an everyday occurrence but a very irregular occurrence, so, unlike interviews where performance can improve with practice, there is little opportunity for practice (unless on a training course) and there is no room for error. The cost of mistakes can be enormous and you may make the situation worse rather than better.

To help diffuse the tension that a manager must inevitably feel, it is worth remembering the following points:

- This is not a win/lose confrontation in which it is 'either you or me'. Remember, it is a process intended to correct undesirable performance and behaviour as quickly as possible. Too often managers see it as a 'winner take all' contest, which raises emotions and produces an ineffective performance.
- The longer you put off confronting the situation the worse it will probably get.
- Good, thorough preparation will increase the chances of success considerably, so, as with all other interviews, *be prepared*.

Before the interview

The first thing you must do is to decide whether to acti-
vate the disciplinary procedure. There is no justification
for setting the wheels in motion just because you have
heard a rumour, or your emotions snap and you feel like
taking it out on someone else. 'Fools rush in where
angels fear to tread,' so, take time to compose yourself
before moving forward.

The first task, if you think the disciplinary procedure
is justified, is to ascertain the reasons for disciplinary
action: the who, what, when, where of the misde-
meanour. If you are to proceed, the facts must be
conclusive and beyond argument. Otherwise, don't
proceed.

During the preparation period, consideration will
have to be given to the style in which the interview is to
be conducted. Apart from the interviewer's style, it will
be very much influenced by the objectives and the stage
reached in the disciplinary process. An interview where
the objective is to correct a minor breach of rules will be
conducted very differently from an interview where the
likely outcome is dismissal. In the former, the atmosphere may well be more akin to a Counselling Interview,
whereas in the latter the atmosphere will be much more
formal with both parties (trades union representative or
work colleague) probably having back-up present.

Other considerations are necessary at the preparation
stage:

- Do not prejudge the outcome of the interview. Your
  job at the interview is to listen carefully to what the
  interviewee has to say. Whilst the facts gathered may
  indicate breach of regulations, when you ask the question 'why' to establish the reasons for the breach, a
  very legitimate reason may emerge.

For example: Joan has been persistently late to work in the past fortnight. By the book, she has been in breach of regulations. The reason for the recent, persistent lateness is that her aged and infirm mother, who lives alone, has recently undergone major surgery and needs attention, particularly in the morning.

A manager concerned with the facts, the application of rules and regulations and who is not prepared to ask questions and listen sympathetically, may just present her with the facts and issue a warning. An alternative and more caring approach would be to conduct the interview by presenting the facts, ascertaining the reasons for the breach of regulations and then exploring options to get around the employee's temporary difficulties. Flexitime, or shortened lunch breaks, may be just two of the options to enable Joan to fulfil her duties to the desired standard.

- Consider the individual you will be interviewing and plan your approach accordingly. Are they sensitive or aggressive? What is likely to be their response? A list of stereotypes and how you might deal with them is given in the exercise at the end of this chapter.

- Whilst you mustn't prejudge the outcome of the interview, you should be clear in your own mind which stage of the disciplinary procedure you have reached, and the possible options open to you. For example, whilst you may have sufficient facts to call the first interview, other things may emerge at this interview that requre further investigation. A possible option is to close the interview pending further enquiries, during which you may decide to suspend the interviewee (usually on full pay) from work pending the investigation. This is a course of action often taken by public sector bodies in the UK such as the police service, the education sector and the health service.

- Make the necessary arrangements regarding the location of the interview. Ensure you have enough privacy and time and take the necessary steps to prevent interruptions from the phone or at the door. Never bawl people out.
- Inform the individual concerned of the time and place of the interview. According to the seriousness of the situation and the stage of the disciplinary procedure, you need to inform the interviewee as to their rights in bringing a representative with them. You should also consider whether you need back-up yourself.

During the interview

Skills required

No interview follows a predictable path, so the interviewer should be prepared for this. Nevertheless, thorough preparation beforehand will increase the likelihood of an effective interview and successful outcome. Again, it is worth stressing that in the majority of cases it is not a confrontation in which winner takes all, but an exploration of an apparent deficiency with the objective of rectifying that deficiency. As an interviewer, the calmer, more composed and less emotional you are, the better your chance of success. As in the Feedback Interview, you must concentrate on the interviewee's *behaviours* and avoid personal criticisms or your own prejudices. The interviewer will probably go through the following stages and display the following skills:

- Establish the purpose of the interview immediately so everyone knows why they are there.
- Briefly state your perception of the situation, which is mainly the presentation of accurate, factual information.

- Give the interviewee the opportunity to state their side of the story. The skilful use of open questions should do this.
- Listen carefully to the responses, probe and summarise where appropriate. This will be interwoven with statements from you about Company rules and regulations and expected standards of performance. The interviewer must be made fully aware of these.
- Come to a decision about a course of action. This will range from help and support to correct a minor performance problem to serving notice of dismissal, according to the stage of the procedure reached. Interviews conducted at the early stage of the procedure should concentrate on alleviating the problem and preventing the procedure from having to go any further. In many cases where dismissal results, the organisation itself must take much of the blame for not ensuring that the problem was dealt with earlier.
- Ensure that at the close of the interview all parties fully understand what the future action is to be.

After the inteview

The following tasks must be carried out:

- Write up your notes *immediately* after the interview whilst everything is fresh in your mind. This will include a record of the interview, the date, who was present, the agreed improvement targets or standards, the consequences of non-improvement in the agreed time, and the support that the interviewer or the organisation will give to achieve the desired outcomes.
- Make a record of any warnings given and send copies to the individual and their representative with copies placed on file.

- Inform the interviewee's trades union or legal representative of any future hearings.
- Fix a time at which to review performance. It may be necessary for the interviewer to spell out exactly what will happen if the agreed performance targets are not met. If the probation period is a long one, then review should not be left until the end, so periodic reviews would be appropriate. After all, if the objective is performance improvement then it is both unfair and counterproductive to let the miscreant go off the rails and use this as ammunition at the next interview.
- Take the necessary action that you agreed with the interviewee to help them rectify the situation.

Exercise 3: The Magnificent Seven

In the following exercise we give descriptions of seven stereotypes who may come before you in a Disciplinary Interview. As part of your preparation, you should have anticipated their reaction to the situation. Suggest ways to deal with these people. (See Appendix IV for our suggestions.)

No.1 Tearful Tina
Tina can turn on the waterworks at will, often mixed with a bit of emotion. Whilst being a keen feminist, in a threatening situation she falls back on her sexuality with the intent of making the interviewer (especially if male) feel very guilty. Most interviewers, particularly men, find such outbursts of emotion very hard to deal with.

No.2 Emotional Edward
Edward doesn't dissolve into tears at interview, but goes into histrionic fits of outrage and indignation. Oh,

the injustice of it! Tantrums and toy-throwing are regularly witnessed. He is being the subject of victimisation and unfair treatment, particularly if the interviewer is female. Provocation and emotional backmail is the agenda and if you let him get away with it he leaves the interview room with even less respect for you than when he entered it.

No. 3 Buck-Passing Brian
The buck never stops with Brian – it's never his fault, it's always someone else's. Brian has a reason for every poor performance or standard – either it's because someone else caused the problem or the system itself is wrong. If only the organisation had listened to his suggestions last year. If only So-and-So had done this. If only the message had got through in time. And why not in the process drop someone else well and truly into the proverbial? And what are *you* going to do about it?

No. 4 Aggressive Angela
Angela dislikes personal criticism and is prone to emotional outbursts. Tall and overpowering, she will try to intimidate by shouting and bursts of indignation. Quick of mind, contemptuous of the organisation and male managers, she knows the Company rules and procedures backwards, as well as her rights, and is likely to give you a full and powerfully delivered exposition of what is wrong around here. If you are meek and mild she will trample all over you. If you are prone to outbursts she'll try to provoke you into losing your temper and dignity.

No. 5 Creepy Colin
Colin is much more stealthy and cunning than Angela. He talks little and listens a lot. Usually you finish up doing all the talking as his silent, apparently uncom-

municative manner creates a void which you feel the need to fill. But the silence is only a snare – the more you talk, the more likely you are to make a mistake and the minute you make one he will pounce with the speed of a cobra and attempt to discredit or destroy your argument.

No. 6 Resigning Reggie

If you listen to Reggie he's had more jobs than you've had hot dinners. That's how much he's in demand and how large is the shortage of people with his skills. Can you really afford to lose him? How is that going to make you look in the eyes of senior management? A man of his talents doesn't have to put up with all this bullshit.

No. 7 Innocent Irene

When you raise the matter with Irene she just flutters here eyelids, saying, 'Surely you are not accusing someone like *me* of doing something like *that*?' Innocent me! You should feel guilty! And apologise!

Summary

Some of the main points in this chapter are:

- In most cases the objective of a disciplinary interview is performance improvement, not punishment.
- Managers conducting disciplinary interviews must always follow the disciplinary procedure of their organisation.
- The organisation should have clearly written down rules and procedures relating to discipline which should be clearly communicated to, and understood by, the workforce and applied consistently.
- An early response to a problem can save an enormous

amount of time, effort and money in the long run. Don't put off confronting the problem.
- Be aware of the facts before confronting the individual and ensure you are fully prepared at the interview:
  - ask open questions
  - listen sympathetically
  - be calm and unemotional and concentrate on behaviours
  - decide on a course of action
  - check for understanding
  - after the interview, write up notes immediately and keep accurate and comprehensive records.

The Exit Interview

People leave organisations on a regular basis. The reason for the departure is either organisation-induced or employee-induced or both. Examples of both are as follows:

> **Organisation:**
> Compulsory retirement
> Redundancy
> Dismissal
> Promotion within a large corporation

> **Individual:**
> Promotion within a large corporation
> Promotion outside the organisation
> Move to another organisation
> Career change
> Retirement

Few organisations conduct an Exit Interview as standard practice. However, in most instances they are beneficial for both the organisation and the individual (the most notable exception being dismissal of either the instant variety or after a series of abortive Disciplinary Interviews). In the dismissal situation there is little to be gained from interviewing the leaver, but nevertheless, the organisation should take the opportunity to learn from the situation. This may result in a review of its disciplinary procedure or a review of its management style, training and development practices, and so on.

The main reason why the exit interview is not

common practice is that both sides often see the other as rejecting *them*. One or both parties therefore avoid confronting a potentially embarrassing situation, blame the other party and dismiss the leaver as 'water under the bridge'. Often each side parts company thinking 'good riddance' or feeling 'very hurt' so that a lot of unresolved emotions exist which for some can take years to come to terms with. With the individual who departs of their own accord, for a position with another organisation, the organisation seeks to sever the umbilical cord as soon as possible. Thus many private sector organisations in the UK often ask employees to clear their desks for immediate departure and pay their salary for the contracted period of notice, in lieu of asking them to work out their notice.

Benefits

The fact that exit interviews are rarely conducted is perplexing since there are many benefits to be gained for both the leaver and the organisation. These can be summarised as follows:

For the organisation

- The individual has reasons for leaving and the organisation should attempt to discover these.
- The Exit Interview marks the start of the recruitment process and information gleaned from the previous incumbent should be taken into account in drawing up job and person specifications for the future.
- In the same way that the Selection Interview is an opportunity for the organisation to sell itself to a potential employee, so the Exit Interview is an opportunity for a good public relations job to be carried out on a future past employee. At worst, it can take the

sting out of a disgruntled employee; at best, it can record appreciation for services rendered and display a caring concern and interest in future success.

- It can obtain valuable feedback on many aspects beyond the job itself, e.g. management style, which can be taken on board to improve the lot of remaining employees.

For the leaver

- They have the opportunity to 'get things off their chest' so that pent-up feelings and aggressions are dispelled early.
- They have the opportunity to make a good ending so that they don't spend time 'looking back in anger' at the time spent in employment with the organisation. Consequently, for the next stage of their career, their emotions and energies can be channelled into positive activities as they make a new start; they don't waste their time harbouring grudges and feeling 'badly done by'.
- They have the opportunity to offer feedback to the organisation, which may result in an improved situation for their successor. The fact that they have been consulted increases the 'feel good' factor.

Nevertheless, despite the advantages for both parties, there are a number of difficulties which must be addressed. These include:

- Both interviewer and interviewee could find the process embarrassing or even traumatic. A lot of bitterness and unresolved emotions may surface. Thought should therefore be given beforehand to the *real* reason for the departure. It may then be felt inappropriate for the immediate line manager to get involved. Alternatives are the upline manager, or someone from the Human Resources Department who should be a skilled interviewer.

• The attitude of the leaver can vary from cooperative to facetious, to emotive, to deliberately misleading.

Great skills is therefore required to deal with the situation and elicit the real reasons for the departure. On the other hand, individuals who are departing the scene are generally more inclined to speak their mind than when they were constrained within the organisation. The interviewer, particularly if it is the immediate line manager, must be prepared for some honest and open feedback which could be both uncomfortable and embarrassing.

Objectives

The main objectives for the interviewer must therefore be as follows:

• to deal with any unresolved emotions
• to make as good an ending as possible for both the organisation and the individual
• to determine the real reasons for the departure with a view to improvement in the future.

The following questions need to be asked at some stage:

1 'What are your main reasons for leaving?'
2 'What did you like about the job?'
3 'What did you dislike about the job?'
4 'Was the training you were given satisfactory?'
5 'How did you find the working conditions?'
6 'What do you think about the wage/salary structure?'
7 'What was your relationship with your manager/ supervisor like?'

The focus in this chapter will be mainly on the individual who is leaving of their own volition to take a position with another organisation. This is not because we intend to ignore the importance of departure for such reasons as redundancy, but because most managers see the exit interview as the result of an individual's departure for another position. Furthermore, as a general rule, emotions and feelings are more to the fore in the redundancy situation, which is better addressed in chapter 4 on Counselling Interviews. But it is important to keep every situation in context and adopt the appropriate behaviours and styles.

Before the interview

A number of tasks need to be undertaken, many of them information-gathering. These are:

- make the appopriate pre-interview arrangements in terms of timing, privacy and furniture arrangements
- find out as much as possible about past performance, attitudes, behaviours, etc.
- find out whether there have been previous attempts to leave. Is the departure part of a carefully planned and executed strategy to move on, or is it merely a spur-of-the-moment over-reaction to something?
- find out if there is a history of grievance or disciplinary action
- confirm whether or not the organisation would want, or be prepared to accept, the withdrawal of notice.
- decide whether to use just the interview or include a questionnaire.

Questionnaires/exit interview forms

The use of questionnaires for any information-collecting exercise can be very helpful. They are a good way of getting the interviewee to open up and can form the basis of an interview or facilitate the opening for the interviewee. Furthermore, many managers feel more comfortable with mechanistic, box-ticking procedures and the questionnaire findings add an element of validity to any statistical analysis. It is beyond the scope of this book to enter into the debate on the pros and cons of using questionnaires and their appropriateness for Exit Interviews. Suffice it to say that many organisations do use them. They could be used in a similar way to reviewing psychometric tests or skills inventories at Feedback Interviews (see chapter 6).

Figure 9.1 gives an example of and Exit Interview questionnaire which can be used or modified as appropriate.

During the interview

Of all the other interviews, the Exit Interview most resembles the Counselling Interview and, to a lesser extent, the Appraisal Interview. The following stages are probably best:

- After initial formalities, time should be allowed to let the leaver feel at ease, to get them ready to talk freely about why they are leaving. But don't go overboard on the settling-in period, otherwise the leaver will start to feel uncomfortable. A skilled interviewer should be able to sense when the time has arrived to move on and start to focus on the task in hand.
- An expression of regret at the leaver's departure followed by a clear statement of the purpose of the interview.
- Explanation from the interviewee of why they are leaving. Leavers may have a lot to get off their chest, in which case the advice is to 'ride out the storm' and

listen carefully. By skilful use of active listening, open questions, summarising and reflecting, the interviewer should be able to get a clear picture. During the interview *do not*:

agree or disagree with either the decision to leave or the reasons given for the decision.

go off at a tangent

interrupt regularly

get emotionally involved

verbally attack the interviewee *whatever the provocation*

be over-preoccupied with your own agenda and seek to 'dig up dirt' about others

- Conclude by thanking the interviewee for their time, repeat the organisation's gratitude for services rendered and wish them every success in the future. Remember, you want the organisation to be held in the best possible light in the leaver's eyes.

After the interview

A number of things need to be done and these include the following:

- The information collected (from the interview and the questionnaire if used) needs to be collated. It is advisable to allow some time to reflect on what has been revealed. It may be of value and truthful, but it may not, so don't take everything at face value. It may be necessary to make further enquiries elsewhere in order to get the full picture.

- The information may have to be incorporated into a report to discover if the leaver's decision is a reflection of a general trend. If so, a clearer picture of the failures (and successes) of the organisation will emerge and the information gathered may be of immense help

Fig. 9.1

CONFIDENTIAL
J. SMITH & SONS LTD

Exit Interview Questionnaire

The aim if the interview, and this form, is to find out the reasons why the employee is resigning. The results will help us to review our policies and practices with the aim of keeping our turnover rate at an acceptable level. We assure you that the information will be kept strictly confidential.

Name	_____	Employee no.	_____
Designation	_____	Date joined	_____
Department	_____	Last working day	_____
Age	_____	Reporting to	_____

A Salary/Employee Benefits

1   The salary is fair compared to your counterparts in similar jobs in other organisations.

Strongly agree   5   4   3   2   1   Strongly disagree

If you disagree, what do you think is a fair amount? _____

2   The salary is fair compared to your peers within the organisation.

Strongly agree   5   4   3   2   1   Strongly disagree

3   You are satisfied with the Company's employee benefits.

Strongly agree   5   4   3   2   1   Strongly disagree

If you disagree, what are you dissatisfied with? _____

4   The salary adjustment granted to you reflects your level of performance.

Strongly agree   5   4   3   2   1   Strongly disagree

5   The promotion prospects in the Company are good.

Strongly agree   5   4   3   2   1   Strongly disagree

B The Job/Working Conditions

1   You like the nature of your job and are satisfied with the duties and responsibilities assigned to you.

Strongly agree   5   4   3   2   1   Strongly disagree

If you disagree, what area did you dislike? _____

_____

2   You are able to handle the work pressure.

Strongly agree   5   4   3   2   1   Strongly disagree

If you disagree, what aspect of your work made it pressured and how can this be managed?

_____

_____

3   You are satisfied with your working hours.

Strongly agree   5   4   3   2   1   Strongly disagree

4   You were given sufficient training opportunities.

Strongly agree   5   4   3   2   1   Strongly disagree

If you disagree, which area(s) was/were lacking?

_____

_____

C Work Relationships
1   You are satisfied with your supervisor in terms of his/her supervisory/ leadership skills.

Strongly agree   5   4   3   2   1   Strongly disagree

2   Your immediate supervisor is fair with subordinates.

Strongly agree   5   4   3   2   1   Strongly disagree

3   Your supervisor shows interest in your welfare and progress.

Strongly agree   5   4   3   2   1   Strongly disagree

4   The working relationship with your peers is generally amicable.

Strongly agree   5   4   3   2   1   Strongly disagree

5   You often receive support from your peers in the department.

Strongly agree   5   4   3   2   1   Strongly disagree

D External Factors   **Please tick reason for your resignation**
1   Better pay and job prospects   [ ]
2   Further studies   [ ]
3   Domestic/family problems   [ ]
4   Distance (too far from home)   [ ]
5   Health reasons   [ ]

Any other comments on your reasons for leaving not reflected above:

_____

_____

Exit Interview Form – Analysis of Scores

The factor with a score of between 5 and 15 is the predominant reason for the employee's resignation. Factors with a score of 16 or above are unlikely reasons for resignation.

Factors   **Score**
A   Salary/employee benefits   [ ]
B   Job/working conditions   [ ]
C   Work relationships   [ ]

_____
Signature of Inteviewer/Date

_____
Signature of Department Manager/Date

in future job design, recruitment, training and career development, remuneration strategies, and so on.

Summary

Many organisations do not carry out exit interviews, so passing up an opportunity to receive valuable feedback on themselves. These interviews should be viewed as a valuable organisational development tool and may provide information that can be acted upon for the benefit of existing and future employees.

The main skills required are the communication skills of open and probing questioning, active listening, summarising and reflecting (see chapter 1). The information gleaned at interviews may be supplemented, where appropriate, by completion of a questionnaire. In many cases the exit interview helps both the organisation and the leaver to make an appropriate ending and forms the springboard for a new start.

Appendix I
Definition of Terms

Key Result Areas (KRAs)
These are the part of the job where the employee can make the greatest contribution to the organisation. Consequently the major effort should be directed at these areas of the job. There are usually about five or six key areas and they help recognise priorities which are often changing.

Standards of Performance or Indicators
These measure success or failure in the job by laying down a minimum level of performance in each of the KRAs. Indicators act as visible signs of progress or problems in a certain area. Examples of possible indicators for some key areas are as follows:

KRA	Indicators (ways to measure)
Sales value (output)	number of units sold number of new units sold versus old units sold market penetration
Maintenance	amount of downtime cost of maintenance per machine maintenance budget – plus or minus ratio of maintenance cost to production cost

Employee satisfaction	number of grievances number of employee complaints number of contributions and suggestions made via a suggestion programme

The most useful indicators are those which highlight problems while there is still time to take corrective action.

Objectives

These are set after both KRAs and indicators of success or failure have been identified. An objective is a precise goal stated in measurable, quantitative and qualitative terms. Remember the acronym, SMART:

S – Specific
M – Measurable
A – Agreed
R – Realistic
T – Time-related

So, if customer satisfaction is a key part of your job, the related objective must be stated specifically enough that you have no problem completing the following statement.

'This task (improving customer satisfaction) will have been satisfactorily performed when the following results have been obtained, or the following conditions have been achieved: …'

KRA	Indicator	Objective
Customer satisfaction	Level of customer complaints	To decrease the level of customer complaints by 10% by [date]

Job description

This should give a clear outline of the aims and objectives of the job. It should clearly state five or six key areas in which results are expected, to ensure personal effectiveness. It should be a short document, clearly stating lines of responsibility and the authority attached to that responsibility.

Organisations and jobs change rapidly in the modern world and so the job description should be reviewed regularly, at least annually. As it underpins all appraisal discussions the annual Appraisal Interview offers a good forum at which to change and update it.

Appendix II

ACAS Code of Practice: Disciplinary Practice and Procedures in Employment

This material is Crown Copyright and is reproduced with the permission of the Controller of Her Majesty's Stationery Office.

A failure on the part of any person to observe any provision of a Code of Practice shall not of itself render him liable to any proceedings; but in any proceedings before an industrial tribunal or the Central Arbitration Committee any Code of Practice issued under this section shall be admissible in evidence, and if any provision of such a Code appears to the tribunal or Committee to be relevant to any question arising in the proceedings it shall be taken into account in determining that question. Employment Protection Act 1975 section 6[11].

Introduction

1   This document gives practical guidance on how to

draw up disciplinary rules and procedures and how to operate them effectively. Its aim is to help employers and trade unions as well as individual employees – both men and women – wherever they are employed regardless of the size of the organisation in which they work. In the smaller establishments it may not be practicable to adopt all the detailed provisions, but most of the features listed in paragraph 10 could be adopted and incorporated into a simple procedure.

Why have disciplinary rules and procedures?

2   Disciplinary rules and procedures are necessary for promoting fairness and order in the treatment of individuals and in the conduct of industrial relations. They also assist an organisation to operate effectively. Rules set standards of conduct at work; procedure helps to ensure that the standards are adhered to and also provides a fair method of dealing with alleged failures to observe them.

3   It is important that employees know what standards of conduct are expected of them and the Contracts of Employment Act 1972 (as amended by the Employment Protection Act 1975) requires employers to provide written information for their employees about certain aspects of their disciplinary rules and procedures.

4   The importance of disciplinary rules and procedures has also been recognised by the law relating to dismissals, since the grounds for dismissal and the way in which the dismissal has been handled can be challenged before an industrial tribunal. Where either of these is found by a tribunal to have been unfair the employer may be ordered to

reinstate or re-engage the employees concerned and may be liable to pay compensation to them.

Formulating policy

5   Management is responsible for maintaining discipline within the organisation and for ensuring that there are adequate disciplinary rules and procedures. The initiative for establishing these will normally lie with management. However, if they are to be fully effective the rules and procedures need to be accepted as reasonable both by those who are to be covered by them and by those who operate them. Management should therefore aim to secure the involvement of employees and all levels of management when formulating new or revising existing rules and procedures. In the light of particular circumstances in different companies and industries trade union officials may or may not wish to participate in the formulation of the rules but they should participate fully with management in agreeing the procedural arrangements which will apply to their members and in seeing that these arrangements are used consistently and fairly.

Rules

6   It is unlikely that any set of disciplinary rules can cover all circumstances that may arise: moreover the rules required will vary according to particular circumstances such as the type of work, working conditions and size of establishment. When drawing up rules the aim should be to specify clearly and concisely those necessary for the efficient and safe performance of work and for the maintenance of satisfactory relations within the

workforce and between employees and management. Rules should not be so general as to be meaningless.

7   Rules should be readily available and management should make every effort to ensure that employees know and understand them. This may be best achieved by giving every employee a copy of the rules and explaining them orally. In the case of new employees this should form part of an induction programme.

8   Employees should be made aware of the likely consequences of breaking rules and in particular they should be given a clear indication of the type of conduct which may warrant summary dismissal.

Essential features of disciplinary procedures

9   Disciplinary procedures should not be viewed primarily as a means of imposing sanctions. They should also be designed to emphasise and encourage improvements in individual conduct.

10   Disciplinary procedures should:

   (a) Be in writing.
   (b) Specify to whom they apply.
   (c) Provide for matters to be dealt with quickly.
   (d) Indicate the disciplinary actions which may be taken.
   (e) Specify the levels of management which have the authority to take the various forms of disciplinary action, ensuring that immediate superiors do not normally have the power to dismiss without reference to senior management.
   (f) Provide for individuals to be informed of the

complaints against them and to be given an opportunity to state their case before decisions are reached.

(g) Give individuals the right to be accompanied by a trade union representative or by a fellow employee of their choice.

(h) Ensure that, except for gross misconduct, no employees are dismissed for a first breach of discipline.

(i) Ensure that disciplinary action is not taken until the case has been carefully investigated.

(j) Ensure that individuals are given an explanation for any penalty imposed.

(k) Provide a right of appeal and specify the procedure to be followed.

The procedure in operation

11 When a disciplinary matter arises, the supervisor or manager should first establish the facts promptly before recollections fade, taking into account the statements of any available witnesses. In serious cases consideration should be given to a brief period of suspension while the case is investigated and this suspension should be with pay. Before a decision is made or penalty imposed the individual should be interviewed and given the opportunity to state his or her case and should be advised of any rights under the procedure, including the right to be accompanied.

12 Often supervisors will give informal oral warning for the purpose of improving conduct when employees commit minor infringements of the established standards of conduct. However, where the facts of a case appear to call for disciplinary

action, other than summary dismissal, the following procedure should normally be observed:

(a) In the case of minor offences the individual should be given a formal oral warning or, if the issue is more serious, there should be a written warning setting out the nature of the offence and the likely consequence of further offences. In either case the individual should be advised that the warning constitutes the first formal stage of the procedure.

(b) Further misconduct might warrant a final written warning which should contain a statement that any recurrence would lead to suspension or dismissal or some other penalty, as the case may be.

(c) The final step might be disciplinary transfer, or disciplinary suspension without pay (but only if these are allowed for by an express or implied condition of the contract of employment), or dismissal, according to the nature of the misconduct. Special consideration should be given before imposing disciplinary suspension without pay and it should not normally be for a prolonged period.

13 Except in the event of an oral warning, details of any disciplinary action should be given in writing to the employee and if desired, to his or her representative. At the same time the employee should be told of any right of appeal, how to make it and to whom.

14 When determining the disciplinary action to be taken the supervisor or manager should bear in mind the need to satisfy the test of reasonableness in all the circumstances. So far as possible, account should be taken of the employee's record and any other relevant factors.

15 Special consideration should be given to the way in
    which disciplinary procedures are to operate in
    exception cases. For example:

    (a) **Employees to whom the full procedure is
        not immediately available**. Special provisions
        may have to be made for the handling of disci-
        plinary matters among night shift workers,
        workers in isolated locations or depots or
        others who may pose particular problems for
        example because no one is present with the
        necessary authority to take disciplinary action
        or no trade union representative is immedi-
        ately available.

    (b) **Trade union officials**. Disciplinary action
        against a trade union official can lead to a
        serious dispute if it is seen as an attack on the
        union's functions. Although normal discipli-
        nary standards should apply to their conduct
        as employees, no disciplinary action beyond an
        oral warning should be taken until the circum-
        stances of the case have been discussed with a
        senior trade union representative or full-time
        official.

    (c) **Criminal offences outside employment**.
        These should not be treated as automatic
        reasons for dismissal regardless of whether the
        offence has any relevance to the duties of the
        individual as an employee. The main consider-
        ations should be whether the offence is one
        that makes the individual unsuitable for his or
        her type of work or unacceptable to other
        employees. Employees should not be dismissed
        solely because a charge against them is pending
        or because they are absent through having been
        remanded in custody.

Appeals

16 Grievance procedures are sometimes used for dealing with disciplinary appeals though it is normally more appropriate to keep the two kinds of procedure separate since the disciplinary issues are in general best resolved within the organisation and need to be dealt with more speedily than others. The external stages of a grievance procedure may, however, be the appropriate machinery for dealing with appeals against disciplinary action where a final decision within the organisation is contested or where the matter becomes a collective issue between management and a trade union.

17 Independent arbitration is sometimes an appropriate means of resolving disciplinary issues. Where the parties concerned agree it may constitute the final stage of procedure.

Records

18 Records should be kept, detailing the nature of any breach of disciplinary rules, the action taken and the reasons for it, whether an appeal was lodged, its outcome and any subsequent developments. These records should be carefully safeguarded and kept confidential.

19 Except in agreed special circumstances breaches of disciplinary rules should be disregarded after a specified period of satisfactory conduct.

Further action

20 Rules and procedures should be reviewed periodically in the light of any developments in

employment legislation or industrial relations practice and, if necessary, revised in order to ensure
their continuing relevance and effectiveness. Any
amendments and additional rules imposing new
obligations should be introduced only after
reaosnable notice has been given to all employees
and, where appropriate, their representatives have
been informed.

Appendix III
Example of a Disciplinary Procedure (any organisation)

From Discipline At Work: ACAS Advisory Handbook. *Reprinted with the permission of ACAS.*

1 Purpose and scope

This procedure is designed to help and encourage all employees to achieve and maintain standards of conduct, attendance and job performance. The company rules (a copy of which is displayed in the office) and this procedure apply to all employees. The aim is to ensure consistent and fair treatment for all.

2 Principles

(a) No disciplinary action will be taken against an employee until the case has been fully investigated.

(b) At every stage in the procedure the employee will be advised of the nature of the complaint against him or her and will be given the opportunity to state his or her case before any decision is made.

(c) At all stages the employee will have the right to be accompanied by a shop steward, employee representative or work colleague during the disciplinary interview.

(d) No employee will be dismissed for a first breach of discipline except in the case of gross misconduct when the penalty will be dismissal without notice or payment in lieu of notice.

(e) An employee will have the right to appeal against any disciplinary penalty imposed.

(f) The procedure may be implemented at any stage if the employee's alleged misconduct warrants such action.

3   The Procedure

Minor faults will be dealt with informally but where the matter is more serious the following procedure will be used:

Stage 1 – Oral warning

If conduct or performance does not meet acceptable standards the employee will normally be given a formal *oral warning*. He or she will be advised of the reasons for the hearing, that it is the first stage of the disciplinary procedure and of his or her right of appeal. A brief note of the oral warning will be kept but it will be spent after ... months, subject to satisfactory conduct and performance.

Stage 2 – Written warning

If the offence is a serious one, or if a further offence occurs, a *written warning* will be given to the employee by the supervisor. This will give details of the complaint, the improvement required and the timescale. It will warn that action under Stage 3 will be considered if there is no satisfactory improvement and will advise of the right of appeal. A copy of this written warning will be kept by the supervisor but it will be disregarded for disciplinary purposes after ... months subject to satisfactory conduct and performance.

Stage 3 – Final written warning or disciplinary suspension

If there is still a failure to improve and conduct or performance is still unsatisfactory, or if the misconduct is sufficiently serious to warrant only one written warning but insufficiently serious to justify dismissal (in effect both first and final written warning), a *final written warning* will normally be given to the employee. This will give details of the complaint, will warn that dismissal will result if there is no satisfactory improvement and will advise of the right of appeal. A copy of this final written warning will be kept by the supervisor but it will be spent after ... months (in exceptional cases the period may be longer) subject to satisfactory conduct and performance.

Alternatively, consideration will be given to imposing a penalty of a disciplinary suspension without pay for up to a maximum of five working days.

Stage 4 – Dismissal

If conduct or performance is still unsatisfactory and the employee still fails to reach the prescribed standards, *dismissal* will normally result. Only the appropriate Senior Manager can take the decision to dismiss. The employee will be provided, as soon as reasonably practicable, with written reasons for dismissal, the date on which employment will terminate and the right of appeal.

4   Gross Misconduct

The following list provides examples of offences which are normally regarded as gross misconduct:

- theft, fraud, deliberate falsification of records, fighting
- assault on another person

- deliberate damage to company property
- serious incapability through alcohol or being under the influence of illegal drugs
- serious negligence which causes unacceptable loss, damage or injury
- serious act of insubordination
- unauthorised entry to computer records

If you are accused of an act of gross misconduct, you may be suspended from work on full pay, normally for no more than five working days, while the company investigates the alleged offence. If, on completion of the investigation and the full disciplinary procedure, the company is satisfied that gross misconduct has occurred, the result will normally be summary dismissal without notice or payment in lieu of notice.

5   Appeals

An employee who wishes to appeal against a disciplinary decision should inform .... within two working days. The Senior Manager will hear all appeals and his/her decision is final. At the appeal any disciplinary penalty imposed will be reviewed but it cannot be increased.

Appendix IV

How to Deal with the Magnificent Seven (Chapter 8)

No. 1 Tearful Tina

Take as long as is necessary for the water supply to dry up. Don't succumb to the emotional blackmail and don't feel guilty or embarrassed and don't apologise. When the emotions have been dealt with, then proceed to the issue and deal with it calmly, unemotionally and rationally. Have your facts to hand and question, don't comment, wherever possible.

No. 2 Emotional Edward

Take as long as necessary to ride out the storm and deal with him in much the same way as you dealt with Tina.

No. 3 Buck-Passing Brian

You must be sure of your facts, so do your homework. Also, anticipate the likely excuses and don't let him wriggle off the hook. Assertively explain the problem and ask him for suggested solutions. Hopefully you will get agreement. If not, you may have to spell it out to him, including the issue of a warning, if merited.

No. 4 Aggressive Angela

As with Tina and Edward, if she has an emotional outburst, ride out the storm. Don't be intimidated and keep your cool. Then deal with her in much the same way as you dealt with Brian.

No. 5 Creepy Colin

Don't let Colin dig a hole for you to jump into. From the beginning get him to talk by using open and probing questions. Don't feel the need to fill any long silences – remember he is the interviewee, not you. Focus on the problem and deal with him in much the same way as you dealt with Brian.

No. 6 Resigning Reggie

If necessary, let him 'get it all off his chest'. Then focus on the problem and deal with him in much the same way as you dealt with Brian. If he feels the need to resign, that must be his decision and obviously you would be sorry to lose him. Be careful you don't say anything that could be interpreted as constructive dismissal.

No. 7 Innocent Irene

Ignore the innocence and stand your ground. Focus on the problem and have your facts to support them. Then deal with her in much the same way as you dealt with Brian.

In short, with all of them you:

- let the emotional storm blow over
- stay calm, collected and unemotional (adult ego state)
- do your homework thoroughly so you have the facts and supporting evidence at your disposal

- question, don't comment
- focus on the problem
- go for joint agreement if possible.

Further Reading

ACAS, *Discipline at Work: The ACAS Advisory Handbook*. HMSO.

Bailey, R., *50 Activities for Developing Counselling Skills*. Gower, Aldershot, 1991.

Berne, E., *Games People Play: The Psychology of Human Relationships*. Grove Press, New York, 1964.

Berne, E., *What Do You Say After You Say Hello?* Grove Press, New York, 1972; Corgi, London, 1975.

Buckman, R., *How to Break Bad News: A Guide for Health Care Professionals*. Macmillan, London, 1992.

Carkhuff, R., *The Art of Helping*. Human Resources Development Ltd, Amherst, 1983.

Denham, W. and Jestico, J., *50 Activities for Appraisal Training*. Gower, Aldershot, 1993.

Egan, G., *The Skilled Helper* (2nd edition). Brooks Kile, Monterey, California, 1962.

Jones, D. and Widdop, D., *34 Activities for Recruitment and Selection*. Gower, Aldershot, 1993.

Mackay, I., *A Guide to Asking Questions*. BACIE, London, 1980.

Mackay, I., *A Guide to Listening*. BACIE, London 1990, second impression.

Pease, A., *Body Language: How to Read Others' Thoughts By Their Gestures*. Sheldon Press, London, 1981.

Pont, T., *Developing Effective Training Skills: A Practical Guide to Designing and Delivering Group Training*, McGraw Hill, Maidenhead, 1996.

Russell, T., *Effective Feedback Skills*. Kogan Page, London, 1994.

Stewart, J. and Cooper, D., *38 Activities for Handling Difficult Situations*. Gower, Aldershot, 1995.

Index

Please send me further information on the range of Training & Development services available. I am particularly interested in:

☐ Management Training Courses

☐ Management Development Consultancy

☐ Psychometric Testing

☐ Counselling Services

Signed _____

Position _____

Company _____

Address _____

_____

_____

Telephone no. _____ Fax no. _____

Please mail to:

Administration Manager

Heyford Associates

Heyford House

Nether Heyford

Northampton

NN7 3NN

United Kingdom

Telephone: +44 - (0)1327-342339

Fax: +44 - (0)1327-349389